THE DUBLIN ROVER

The Dublin Rover

by

SÉAMUS SCULLY

From the library of
Danny Doyle
Raised on songs and stories

TARA BOOKS • DUBLIN

This book was set by
Seton Music Graphics, Bantry,
for Tara Books,
an imprint of Irish Academic Press Ltd,
Kill Lane, Blackrock, Co. Dublin.

ACKNOWLEDGEMENTS

The essays in this book were read by Séamus Scully to the Old Dublin Society,
and later published in *Dublin Historical Records* as follows:
1. Ghosts of Moore Street: read on 17 Febr. 1971;
   in *DHR*, Vol XXV. No. 2, March 1972.
2. Around Historic Naul: read on 27 March 1979;
   in *DHR*, Vol. XXVIII, No. 3, June 1975.
3. Around Dominic Street: read on 7 March 1979;
   in *DHR*, Vol. XXXIII, No. 3, June 1980.
4. Rotunda Gardens and Buildings: read on 1 March 1971 ['81?];
   in *DHR*, Vol. XXXIV, No. 3, June 1981.
5. Moore Street, 1916: read on 14 Dec. 1983;
   in *DHR*, Vol. XXXIX, No. 2, March 1986.
6. The Abbey Theatre 1916 Plaque: read on 27 March 1986;
   in *DHR*, Vol. XLIII, No. 4, Sept. 1988.
7. Dublin's Historic Hollywood: read on 15 March 1989;
   in *DHR*, Vol. XLIII, No. 1, Spring 1990.

British Library Cataloguing in Publication Data
Scully, Seamus
The Dublin rover
I. Title
941.8350824

ISBN 0 7165 2480 5

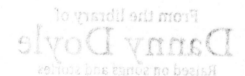

Printed in Ireland
by Colour Books Ltd, Dublin

For Mercy has a human heart
Pity a human face:
And Love, the human form divine,
And Peace, the human dress,
    . . .

(from "The Divine Image"
by William Blake)

Contents

Introductory Note

In the year 1991, when Dublin is in the limelight as Cultural Capital of Europe, it is appropriate to pay tribute to its culture with this collection of essays originally read by Séamus Scully to the Old Dublin Society over the last two decades.

Mr Scully, more familiarly called Séamus, and even more popularly known as Jimmy, is a true-born Dubliner who has made himself a local historian, a walking encyclopaedia about people, places, sayings and events of his native city and surroundings. He has reached the venerable age of 81, but he is still as lively, inquisitive and buoyant as a child. Not long ago, we happened to listen to one of his soliloquies about how nice it would be

> when I die, to have some of my scattered papers published in one volume, just to help people not to forget the places I have written about . . . and not to forget me. . . .

This publication is a tribute to the field work of Séamus Scully alive, to a man of culture who knows Dublin like the back of his hand and who is himself a most intriguing introduction to Irish culture (as effectively shown in Garret Keogh's first documentary, of his series of seven, *Old Heads*, broadcast on RTE 2 on Thursday, 9 November 1989).

Culture as embodied by Séamus Scully is cultivation of the mind in response to the needs of individual intellectual curiosity and, as a natural follow-up, production of knowledge by sharing the fruit of one's own knowledge with the community.

Octogenarian Séamus remains an impenitent mental as well as physical traveller, who keeps ignoring the static dimension and only enjoys the notion of dynamics. Despite the "small" ulcer on his leg, however safe and comfortable his abode (a rented bedsitter in a compound for old-age pensioners, which he was lucky to find in 1986, after a lifetime spent in hundreds of digs), he is still a rambler, an inquisitive and hearty rover, still much in demand among the "An Óige" people. Some of his old friends enjoy quoting by heart the parody in verse, "Ode to the Great Scully", by Tony Butler (he, too, familiarly called Jimmy, like his friend Scully), a respected journalist and critic, who died recently:

ODE TO THE GREAT SCULLY

Who forms excursions for the *ard craobh* clan,
Who but that famous wonderful man — Scully.

Who makes them jolly and really happy,
Who but that perfect splendid chappy — Scully.

Who never lets us miss a train,
Who guides and keeps us from every pain — Scully.

When Stephen fell into the brine, poor boy,
Who gently scolded him and wiped his tearful eye — Scully.

When Mairéad was naughty, the saucy miss,
Who soothed her with a fatherly kiss — Scully.

Who never shouts or calls us young rips,
Who but that hero of a hundred trips — Scully.

> So raise your voices in cheer
> For *Ard Craobh*'s pet,
> For *Ard Craobh*'s dear — SCULLY!

When he was young, he was a clerk at Irish Shell and proved himself to be "a born organiser" in the twelve years when he ran, as Secretary, the famous Technical Students' Literary and Debating Society, in Parnell Square. Many people in Dublin, on the island, and overseas still have a vivid memory of his "sturdy, keen, copper-haired young Dubliner" who, through his charming (not rarely pressing) invitations, was able to have his Saturday-evening debates presided over by the most prominent figures of the time in the fields of politics, literature, diplomacy, theatre, religion, social sciences, and current affairs in general.

As soon as he got a room of his own at 27, Ballybough Court, Dublin 3, he made his "*little* room an everywhere" open to any one in search of information unavailable in institutional repositories—rare books, theatre programmes, photographs (most of them autographed and annotated), newspaper cuts, letters, mementos (including locks of hair belonging to historical figures), and—more precious than anything—the living memory of facts and figures stored in his old (?) head as fresh as a rose. Here is an excerpt from one of his letters, written to me on 18 April 1986:

> Did I mention to you that I have at last got a senior citizen flat which at the moment I am having redecorated. It is in Ballybough, right in the heart of the city, convenient to Fairview. A large bedsitter, with separate toilet and kitchenette, and I have a balcony, on which I will get much sun in Summer, and have been told to get a deck chair. So that is good news, so you can often come to me for meals that you like and can prepare. . . .
>
> Will not be moving in for a few weeks, so you can continue to write to me here. I also hope to have a phone installed. . . . I still have some books for you. And I can make plenty of shelves for mine in the flat—in fact, now I am sorry I sold so many, but still have much good ones on hand.

Yes, a longed-for room with a view, a shelter for the man and his books, yet nothing but a release point for "the scholar gipsy". In the same letter he says:

> I shall be looking forward to your Summer visit and am willing to go with you anywhere on holiday . . . and still have so many friends for you to visit. However, I am at your disposal for anything you so desire. There are so many hostels around Galway that I have still to visit, particularly Carna, which is a really Irish-speaking area.

Five years later, Séamus Scully is still on the move. Since the early '30s, he has been an undaunted theatregoer (and dressing-room visitor as a follow-up to each performance), an indefatigable reference-digger in libraries and archives, a resolute reaper of records, relics, oral and written reports, all of them detected with sagacity and handled with loyalty. He still remains a most resourceful dispenser of culture through his public talks, papers, letters to newspapers, correspondence with his numerous interlocutors (world-famous scholars, obscure researchers, high politicians, men and women of the street, old-time friends, youths and children scattered over Ireland and overseas). But the most enjoyable, exciting, and enriching cultural experience of all is Séamus Scully's "river-run" talk over a cup (more than one cup) of tea, indoors or in the open air, poured out of his flask, the Dublin rover's lifelong companion.

Love for knowledge, love for *shared knowledge*, pursued with mental integrity and human participation: this is the stuff Séamus Scully is made of. And because this is the stuff culture is made of, I am glad to be associated with this publication in the context of Dublin as Europe's Capital City of Culture, and to wish him many happy returns in his beloved native city, where I first met him in 1983, when he gave his lecture on "Moore Street 1916" to the Old Dublin Society.

ROSANGELA BARONE

Réamhrá

Stair atá beo atá anseo ó staraí beoga.
Go maire sé a chéad leabhar.

Some historians impose themselves on their subjects, on the locales, and issue solemn nostrums from the dung-heaps of their arrogance. They are the transient scents of fashion and of puffed fame: and they give history a bad name.

Séamus may, "Ancient Mariner"-like, impose his stream of lore, but, as it flows about, you are neither drowned nor drenched, but rather enchanted and enhanced by the experience. If occasionally in the broader sweeps modern recensions seem to be ignored it is not that important really: they are the frame only, not the line and the colour that he evokes of people in place and place as setting.

Séamus is a celebrator, a recaller with affection, a recorder with love: and obviously a man who enjoys the hunt and the chase, the search itself, the tracing from half-leads—one who delights in the very sounds and smells of the past, who remembers the shape of a fanlight, the colour of a hall-door, and who can still squirm with embarrassment as he remembers Jim Larkin's derogatory comments about his own beloved Moore Street.

He is a north Dublin man—if I said "north city" I'd ignore the essays which explore Dublin's Hollywood and The Naul for us, making them redolent of their own past, their hidden histories, and telling us of the quirks and turns of time they fared through. This is delightful local history at its best— and the thematic, schematic, synoptic histories, to be history, must really be based on solid foundations of local experience faithfully reproduced and understood, on the cherished minutiae of local history.

Nineteen ninety-one, too, is, of course, the 75th anniversary of 1916—*Bliain na Cinniúna*—the year when "All changed, changed utterly", the year of the Proclamation of

the Republic, and the year when the defeated upholders of
the Republic retreated from their HQ at the GPO through
Séamus's own street: and hence the republication here of this
"Moore Street 1916" (which I heard in 1983 as a lecture to
the Old Dublin Society, and which has only improved with
the passing of time) is very appropriate, a reminder of how
1916 was experienced, how it changed lives, how it deep-
ened them.

The theatre is another love of Séamus's, and O'Casey—a
friend—comes in and out of these essays: he even arrives at
The Naul.

And perhaps it is in the article on the plaque in the Abbey
Theatre, commemorating the seven from the company who
took part in the Rising, that Séamus is seen at his best.
There, good historian as he is, he confesses failure in his
efforts to find out about one of them—a stage-hand; he
evokes much of the atmosphere of the Dublin of the time in
the vignettes on Máire Nic Shiúbhlaigh, Arthur Shields and
Helena Molony especially. But best of all is his celebration of
the sometime usherette Nellie Bushell, who gave him his first
pass to his first play in the Abbey, her role in the Marrowbone Lane in 1916, her life back in the theatre when it was
over, and the loneliness of her death despite "the rattling of
the blank bullets and the mournful dirge of the Last Post"
that marked her burial.

Go n-éirí leat, a Shéamuis, tá muid faoi chomaoin agat.
Leabhar eile anois?

PÁDRAIG Ó SNODAIGH

1

Ghosts of Moore Street

Moore Street—that famous marketing venue, with its numerous butcher shops, its noisy women dealers and their colourful stalls, is known to us all. It is possible that there is even one Dubliner who has not passed down this busy marketing place? One never queries Moore Street, but takes it for granted that it has always been there; but ask, even those who reside in it, from whence it derived its name, and most will plead ignorance, or surmise that it was called after the famous Irish poet. But, like so many of our Dublin streets, it was christened after a family of adventurous Planters, who crossed from England to make their fortune at the expense of the native Irish, and this family succeeded in procuring half a dozen monasteries for their descendants.

The brothers Moore arrived in our country in the middle of the 16th century; and Edward, the more ambitious, was successful in his petition of 1565 in obtaining from the Tudor Elizabeth the already plundered Abbey of Mellifont and its surrounding land "to him and his posterity for ever". He converted the Abbey itself into a fortress, utilising the church as a "spacious and defensible mansion", which we learn from documents of that period "was very necessary for the inhabitants in time of insurrection and attack by the Irish attempting to prey on the country". Another unsuccessful candidate at the same time, for the Abbey, was the Northern chieftain, Shane O'Neill, who had pleaded to the Queen "for the Lordship of Mellifont that he may dwell there as all his property has been destroyed and that he required a wife of the English nation, to increase his civil education, and cause his followers to acknowledge their duty to the Queen".

On Edward Moore's death the property passed to his son, Garrett (or Gerald) and it was here at Mellifont, on 29 March 1603, that the great Hugh O'Neill knelt in submission to Elizabeth before him and the Lord Deputy Mountjoy, unaware that the Queen was already three days dead. It was the lamentable beginning of the Flight of the Earls, and the collapse of the old Gaelic Order. It is obvious that Sir Garrett had previously formed a friendship with O'Neill, probably at the English Court, as we know that O'Neill had been educated in that country and in the Protestant faith, and when he returned to Ireland, he was regarded by the Government not alone as having English sympathies but also as a Protestant. Sir Garrett was also foster-father to O'Neill's son, John, and this alliance was regarded as stronger than blood.

In 1619, the now Baron Moore was to receive another plundered grant, that of Dublin's Saint Mary's Abbey, the lands of which extended from the edge of the Liffey to the present Broadstone extending to the River Tolka. Before its desecration by order of Henry VIII, it was regarded as the richest and most sumptuous in the Kingdom, and then it had been in existence for over 500 years. A small portion of it is still preserved down a miserable lane off Capel Street. When Garrett Moore died, in 1628, it is estimated that he was the possessor of over 50,000 acres around his Manor at Mellifont.

He was followed by his son, Charles, who was to play an important part in the resistance against the so-called "rebels" at the siege of Drogheda in 1642, which lasted for over six months. He lost his life at the battle of Portlester, near Trim, in 1643, against Owen Roe O'Neill, to the cry of "Lámh Dhearg Abu!" We now read a pleading—or begging—letter from his widow to Charles I for the advancement of her teenage son, Henry, who is the chief interest of this paper. In a short time we find that he has been created Governor of Meath and Louth, but on the collapse of the Government to Cromwell, his estates are sequestrated; after the Restoration he is elevated to the earldom of Drogheda.

The Moores had made the Abbot's house at Saint Mary's Abbey their city residence, until early in the 18th century, when portion of the land, which was called by the monks "Ash Park", was laid out for building purposes from which, around 1728, arose Drogheda Street, now O'Connell Street; and later came Earl Street, Henry Street and Moore Street; all of which were called after the first Earl of Drogheda. At this time Drogheda Street was but a narrow thoroughfare extending from a country road (now called Parnell Street) down to where stands the present GPO, then almost lapped by the River Liffey, which could only be crossed by a ferry. The nearest bridge was then at Capel Street—which was the most fashionable street in the City. Twenty-five years yet to pass before the foundation stone was laid, by the Lord Mayor, of Dr Bartholomew Mosse's Lying-in hospital—the first of its kind in Europe "on the lease of waste ground with a pool in the hollow, and a few cabins on the slope." Its gardens were to become the aristocratic amusement grounds of the city; and its dignified surrounding buildings in 1792 housed eleven peers, two bishops and eleven Members of Parliament. At this time Dublin was regarded as the second city of the Empire. The Earl had now erected his palatial Drogheda House at the corner of Mellifont Lane (now Cathedral Street) with its elegant fountain splashing into Drogheda Street. The plaque on the house at present does not commemorate the Earl of Drogheda, but one who fell in civil strife against brother Irishmen. Drogheda Street was to retain that name for 28 years.

The first advertisement I find of Moore Street is dated September 1719, in the *Freeman's Journal*. I feel that I must quote it in full because of its simplicity and delightful wording. It is signed by one Benjamin Higgins:

> John Lowry, my servant, left his service on Tuesday last, without the least cause or provocation. As he was easy tempered, it is supposed he was wheeled away by some evil-minded person. He went off in a coat and waist-coat of dark brown cloth with livery buttons, the coat lined with red serge and a red collar, with fustain breeches. His hat laced with narrow silver lace, and silver shoe buckles. He is about 16 years old, marked with small-pox, with light hair and tender eyes. If he submissively returns to his duty in a reasonable time, he will be forgiven, and I hope no gentleman or other person will employ him, as he is my indentured apprentice.

I was unable to trace if youthful John returned to his Moore Street abode, but I like to think that he wandered away in that distant past with a dainty maiden in a colourful crinoline.

A few years later I find that there is a Mr Andrew Gardiner lodging with a Mrs Hussey of Moore Street, who

classifies himself as an "operator of teeth" and whose quali-
fications must make his present-day profession feel more than
a little jealous. He has what he calls an infallible specific named
"Dentrisic Albaitor", a box of which perfectly whitens the
teeth and preserves them, cures the scurvy and gives a natural vermilion colour to the gums; and it only costs 2s.8½d.
per box. He also claims to clean and scale the teeth and to
render the blackest perfectly white and beautiful in less than
an hour, and can place artificial teeth with the greatest of
nicety: that people may eat, drink and sleep with them in
their mouths, and use them in common as natural ones—
from which they cannot be discovered by the sharpest eye.
He fills hollow teeth with gold or lead, and fastens loose teeth
in their sockets.

At the same time there is a Mr Andrew McMahon of the
Coffee Bar and Chocolate Warehouse in Moore Street, near
Henry Street, advising us that he has engaged a London
chocolate expert "and that Ladies or Gentlemen who have a
peculiar flavour for Chocolate, by sending notices before-
hand, can have quantity and quality made to their taste."

And then there is a Mr J. H. Brier, who has his business at
13 Moore Street, informing us that he has claret that is now
two years in the bottle at 1½ guineas per dozen, and that
they will speak their own eulogy.

In May of 1764 we read in the newspaper that Mr Edward
Foy of Moore Street, Sedan Chairmaker, has taken unto wife
a Miss Welch of Cole's Lane, and that the sacred ceremony
took place at night. Funerals at night were the common
practice at this period; but I wonder was this marriage excep-
tional and also wonder how many of the Mr Foy's sedan
chairs jostled around the Rotunda amusement grounds and
down Drogheda Street; and did one of the Moore earls relax
in their comfort.

In February 1767, we find a gentleman interested in the
hygiene of his native city, who signs himself "B.C.", writing
angrily about a "Refuse heap" to "The Committee for con-
ducting the Free Press":

> Gentlemen, An ingenious writer has mentioned, and
> daily experience verifies, that the laws were made for
> the little. One instance I beg leave to give you.

Curiosity led me every day for a week, lately, to the Lying-in hospital through Moore Street: wherein, near Britain Street, lies a dunghill or heap of rubbish of about twenty yards in length—terminated by a butcher's stall—whereby that part of the street is rendered almost impassible in wet weather; and the small part of the pavement which is uncovered by the rubbish seems to have been a long time neglected. I had curiosity to enquire in the neighbourhood why this nuisance was suffered etc., and was informed that it has remained nearby in the same condition for upwards of three years, notwithstanding many applications of the inhabitants of Moore Street to persons whose province it was to redress them. But the reason given me why such applications were fruitless was this: that the ground on which the rubbish lies and the neglected pavement belong to a gentleman of fortune. I am, Gentlemen, your humble servant.

And in August of the same year, an individual who conceals his identity under the nom-de-plume "Pro Bono Publico" complains of a more serious matter, some "Presentiments for sewers to be made in Moore Street; which, though of a private nature were endeavoured to be built at the public expense, and for no less than £250, which, if he was rightly informed, would not be quarter sufficient to finish the job; notwithstanding the money levied for the same purpose last year." The sewer pipes have caused more than a flutter in the Wardens' dove cots, for the following advertisement appears in the paper a few days later. "The Church-Wardens of Saint Brigid's, tenacious of the rights of their fellow citizens, request a Meeting with other Church-Wardens of the different parishes in this city at the Half Moon in Big Ship Street on Wednesday next at 6 in the evening, in order to promote to prosecuting of a traverse to some presentments which are thought to be an imposition on the Public." I was unable to find the verdict of this Church-Warden gathering.

Three years later, those who indulge in the "light fantastic" find themselves in difficulty—just like our modern youth, they have disturbed the slumbering neighbours: "The inhabitants of Moore Street request the Supervisors of the Watch

of Saint Mary's parish will be pleased to take notice of a
house in Moore Street known by "The Sign of the Shoulder
of Mutton" wherein is held a club or meeting of Gentlemen's
servants three nights every week, and who, on their depar-
ture, abuse every innocent person they meet to the great terror
and disturbance of said inhabitants. N.B. Said house goes
under the denomination of a dancing school". The next
month "The Shoulder of Mutton" is again before the public
and the following appears in the Press:

> The inhabitants of Moore Street present their respect-
> ful compliments to the Rt. Hon. Lord Mayor and beg
> his Lordship will be pleased to take notice of a butcher's
> stall near the house that goes under the denomination
> of the Servant's Dancing School, at the sign of "The
> Shoulder of Mutton", and request his Lordship will
> have it removed out of said Street, being a very great
> nuisance in the day and a lodgment in the night for the
> miscreants that endanger the lives and properties of the
> said inhabitants and passengers.

I regret that I have been unable to obtain any further
information of "The Shoulder of Mutton"'s activities.

Dubliners, I am sure, will be amazed to learn that Moore
Street once had the distinction of having a hospital—the first
of its kind in the British Dominions. It was opened in 1818,
under the title of the Dublin Infirmary of Cutaneous Dis-
orders, and later changed to the more simple "The Dublin
Infirmary for Curing Diseases of the Skin"—and was located
in No. 20. It was maintained at the private expense of a Dr
William Wallace, MD MRIA MRSI, who was surgeon at Jervis
Street Infirmary, and who resided at 4 Great Denmark Street.
(His next-door neighbour, at No. 3, was Lord Norbury.) It
ceased to function after his death in 1837. During the period
of its existence it had dealt with 22,000 patients. I have been
unable to trace where this generous-hearted surgeon is
buried, and would like to think that a tombstone is inscribed
to his humane work for the poor of Dublin; and grieve to
think that like his philanthropic predecessor—Dr Mosse—he
should lie in an unknown grave.

As early as 1819 we find Messrs Hampton Leedom, Soap
Boiler and Chandler, at 34/35 Moore Street—who are the

sole agents for University Candles; six more years were to pass before Dublin was to be lit by gas. In 1820 we learn that this firm "presented the Society for the Suppression of Mendicity with a quantity of soap to be given to the Spinners of the district, in compliment of their increasing cleanliness." Later these premises moved to Henry Street; and it was here that a defective-sighted poor young lad got his first job; and who was later to rock Dublin with his plays of city tenement life. How often must little Johnny Cassidy, as he was then called, have run up and down Moore Street, in his leaking boots from No. 20 Dominick Street Lower, then a Protestant school in which his sister was a teacher; and is now Saint Saviour's Orphanage, with its beautiful Georgian ceilings and plaster work.

In 1835, we find that No. 7 Moore Street has a school conducted by Mrs Susanna Prentice, and the following year it has been extended to a Boarding School under the supervision of Miss Supple. And also in the same building Mr Hickey runs his Brush Manufacturing business. A few doors down, at No. 15, is Miss Anne Scoles' stationery shop and Circulating Library. Had the dear lady any naughty books under the counter for the gay dancers at the "Shoulder of Mutton"? Six years later, at No. 28 we find the home of Miss Alicia Mary Murray, also the English and French School run by Miss Emily Macklin; and, in addition, a bakery run by Mr Patrick Fitzpatrick, apparently all content in the one building.

During the horrifying famine of 1847, when starvation stalked the land and thousands were dying by the roadside or fleeing from the plague in the coffin ships—which cast a shadow over the national mind flickering even to this generation—in this year in Moore Street we find 62 shops of which only nine were butchers, but 41 of the others were dealing in food. At No. 39 resided George Bonner, who was victualler to the Lord Lieutenant. In No. 24 was John Behan, fishmonger to the same gentleman. William Flemming was at 41—a cheese and pickle and Italian merchant to his Excellency. Moore Market, now almost in shambles, had 13 shops all dealing in food—two of which supplied his Excellency with fish. The present insignificant Riddles Row had 27 houses, which contained 32 butchers' shops or stalls, and Mr John Ryan at No. 1 had the honour of supplying meat to his Excellency.

The Dublin Season, noted for its gaiety and extravagance, was as lively as ever this year, and the Lord Lieutenant, Lord Bessborough as the Queen's Deputy still maintained the Dublin Court in semi-royal pomp at the Castle; even though he had been complaining of not being in "the best of health, due to the Balls and Drawing-Rooms which had knocked him up". On 16 May the press reports that he "breathed his last peacefully and without a struggle, and the sad event will cast a gloom over the whole country, and hand down his name to posterity as a true patriot and benefactor to his native land". But after his spectacular funeral the gay life continued, and business at Moore Street was as active as ever, just as if the country's life was normal.

Fifty years later, the beauty of her day, Miss Maude Gonne, who had been presented at the English Court, mentioned in her address in vigorous French to an audience of 1,200 at the Luxembourg University:

> It is but 50 years ago, but it still lives in thousands of memories. Men and women ate the dogs, the cats, the rats, the grass of the fields, and some even, when all the food was gone, ate dead bodies. I have been told it by women who had heard the last sigh of their dying children without being able to lessen their agony with one drop of milk. I am adding nothing to mournful reality.

In later years she was to hold more vigorous meetings against threatened removal of the Moore Street dealers from the street. In old age, but with slight remains of her beauty and now a gaunt ghost-like figure clad in fluttering black, she addressed fiery political rallies in face of military attack, on the shattered rubble scattered on the site of the one-time Drogheda Mansion of the Moore earls—in what is now called O'Connell Street.

Moore Lane, up to 1773, had been called Brickfield Lane, and in 1840 it is interesting to note that it housed the following businesses:—Office of Robert Hamilton & Co., solicitors; Office of Maxwell Hamilton, Crown Solicitors, North East Circuit, and Solicitors to the Dublin Police Establishment; Office of Robert Simpson, Solr., Marshall of the High

Court of the Admiralty; and the Offices of James Pratt, Deputy Sergeant at Arms. For several years around 1983 it housed the *Freeman's Journal*, Printers and Publishers. To us kids it was known as Marble Lane because, from the rubbish thrown out from the mineral water factory, we collected glass marbles amongst the broken mineral water bottles, which were used as stoppers in place of the present metal caps.

On October 1894 we again find the residents of Moore Street complaining—this time to the Dublin Corporation about its neglected condition. They grumble that "the Street is one of the principal thoroughfares from the Broadstone Station, but owing to the fact that it is so badly paved, the Cab and Car drivers of the city purposely avoid it." And the "residents also consider that the electric light at present in Mary Street and Henry Street might be extended to Moore Street when it is realised what an important thoroughfare and market Moore Street is." As a result of a deputation to the Paving and Lighting Committee, we find in the press of the following February "that work has begun of lighting Moore Street with electricity" and the only thing that they desire further "is that repaving should commence as soon as possible, that it is a palpable necessity and deserves the immediate attention of the Corporation". In *Thom's Directory* of this year, for the first time, appears the name of George Scully at 31 Moore Street, who is classified as the sole "Purveyor" in the street. This is destined to be my home for 25 years covering the 1916 Rising, the Black and Tans, and the Civil War.

Our shop was but one house from Britain Street, so I had a front Dress Circle view from our parlour window of the daily life at that corner. I am now wondering was it outside our house that lay that "manure heap" referred to by the angry "B.C." "in Moore Street near Britain Street" in the dim past of 1767.

On Saturday nights, after I was washed by carbolic soap in the clumsy zinc bath before the blazing kitchen range (like the rest of the street we had no bathroom, and what was referred to in a muffled tone as the WC was down in the cellar almost under the iron street railings) I was wrapped in a tartan woollen-haired rug and propped up in the parlour arm-chair close to the windows, but not too far from the glowing fire, for fear that I might catch a chill, and allowed to peep out under the tasselled fringe of the blind, at the whirling world below. Horse-drawn vehicles pranced and clattered on the skiddy cobblestones to the abusive shouts of the confused drivers trying to avoid the surging mass of shoppers who swelled out from the crowded paths on to the slimy rubbish of the roadway. Along Britain Street clanked the cumbersome swaying tramcars, their jerking trolleys spluttering coloured sparks from the overhead shiny steel wires, and their iron wheels thudding and grinding over the shrieking iron rails.

Opposite us was the tiny one-storied poultry shop, quaintly numbered 30½, as if it had been wedged in between its own adjacent neighbours. Old Christy and his sons were busy selling flour-powdered chickens and scarlet skinned rabbits from the cracked marble topped tables, and his daughters were titivating (more to come) behind the wooden partition at the back of the shop, and occasionally giving a transient glance at the bargaining customers. The previous day, to my delight, I had seen the live fowl hauled into the shop from the two-tiered wooden-crated cart, fluttering, cackling and chuckling, and I hoped that one would escape, to be chased in its awkward flight over the dealers' stall by the frightened women.

To-morrow I expected to see the old man squeeze out through the shutters of the closed shop in his bright green and dazzling gold uniform, with its dangling sword, topped with the white curved ostrich feathered hat to attend the Foresters' Parade at Parnell Square. The previous Sunday I had been disappointed as he emerged in his ordinary Sunday suit, wearing something green in his button-hole, which I heard Father say to my brothers were Ivy Leaves and that he was off to a meeting at Parnell Monument. Next year four of his sons were to leave that little poultry shop and shoulder their rifles in what the neighbours called "the Rebellion". One was never to return. He died manning the barricades in Church Street. On the original Abbey Programme of *The Plough and the Stars* one of the Volunteers is classified as a "Chicken Butcher". O'Casey told me that he had forgotten the name of that Volunteer. But I am happy to think that poor Pad Joe is remembered.

Underneath the parlour was our shop and I could faintly hear Father's voice and his assistants' bargaining with the women over the price of pigs cheeks, back bones and ribs, which were being sold from the pickle barrels. Then I could hear them being cackled and hammered on the large wooden block at the end of the shop, to be eventually wrapped up in newspaper. Some of these goods I could see down below on the tables beside the picnics and the white-salted bacon called "the lad", and dangling overhead were the flitches of bacon and the dried ling fish, all haphazardly guarded by the whistling messenger-boy in his knickerbocker trousers. On my left I could barely see Farrington's shop, which only sold bread and it steaming hot: and the poor dealers readily sought the cheap split loaves at 2¼d. each.

On my right below I could barely see the tables of the butcher's shop, laden with chunks of corned beef and red-blocked sliced meat of various cuts. Whilst under the tables lay the sheeps' and cows' heads dripping with blood—and with their stark eyes—which a few days previously had been driven up the street by the shouting drovers, followed by yelling youngsters beating animals with sticks, to the slaughter houses behind the shops in the surrounding lanes. We called them the Lime yards, as they were frequently dashed and washed with lime to deaden the stench of manure and blood. Here the kids grabbed the freshly killed pigs' bladders—blew them out and when dry used them as "footballs". The older folk afflicted with chilblains and similar complaints, waded, for a cure, in the animal manure. Others sought the animals' gall for the washing of heavy clothing, and it was also used in the paper business for the ruling of lines.

In the Summer evenings, how I envied the barefooted children, and I imprisoned in my room, as they romped around their mothers who were perched on upturned boxes behind their stalls, and their prattling voices joining their parents' in shouting out their goods for sale, in the evening sun. But the Winter was different, to see the same children and they shivering in their tattered clothes with blue feet and legs, clinging to their mother's skirts and seeking the scanty shelter under their flimsy shawls from the sleety winds; at odd times gulping mouthfuls of tea from crude cracked jugs, their pallid faces made more sickly-looking by the flickering gas light of the surrounding shops. Little did my childish mind, in the midst of pampered comfort, as I watched the mothers load their unsold goods on to the perambulators, realize, as they cautiously pushed them along followed by their shivering children,the scanty meal that awaited in their bleak Dominick Street homes—once the stately residences of the wealthy, with their lofty rooms, decorated ceilings, and delicate Bossi fireplaces, now the dismal draughty tenements, the tombs of Dublin's poor.

In 1915 we find that there are now no butchers' shops in the one time popular Riddles Row and Moore Market, they have apparently transferred into Moore Street, which now has 20 butchers shops. The shops in the lanes now deal in second-hand furniture, clothing, and footwear, many of the so-called houses should be pulled down—they are in such a deplorable condition, and with dreadful sanitary conditions. For example, Norfolk Market has only two water closets for seventeen families, and an iron hand pump in the middle of the lane the sole water supply. Some years later I was embarrassed and ashamed to hear "Big Jim Larkin" refer to "the slums surrounding Moore Street" as the worst in Dublin.

It is 1916. For two years war has been booming over Europe. Mighty powers are battling to decide the fate of small nations. It is 29 April and almost 3.30. For almost a week in Dublin there has been destruction, bloodshed and death. It has been a continuous nightmare. The General Post Office is a blazing volcano, Henry Street is in flames that are consuming the houses in Moore Street, which is clouded in grimy rank smoke. A British barricade has been mounted at the end of the street and stretches out into Britain Street, and with its heavy artillery has already played havoc with the buildings and taken many lives. It is almost beneath the window of No. 31, where three little frightened boys are huddled in the corner of the room, in fear of that window; already bullets have darted through the rooms overhead, and a few doors up the street a butcher's wife has been shot dead in her room at the corner of Riddles Row, by a stray bullet. For nearly an hour the street has been silent—a frightening silence—and now from their safe corner the awestricken boys can see through that window a fluttering white flag with a red cross; it is carried by a nurse and beside her briskly walks a clean-shaven soldier, neatly dressed in a green uniform, they both halt at the barricade, he salutes a British officer, hands over his sword and hurriedly glances up the burning street, and they both pass through an opening in the barricade. Some time later, down the street is carried a stretcher by six green-uniformed Volunteers, and the little boys can see lying on it a figure in a different coloured uniform: it is blackish grey—the stretcher halts for a few moments outside the little poultry shop, then the barricade is reopened and the seven solemn figures pass out of view into Britain Street. Little did those startled schoolboys realize that they were witnessing one of the most pathetic pages of Irish history—the surrender, or suppression, but not defeat, of an ancient nation. For almost a week it had braved the might of an Empire to preserve its individuality. That fight would alter the course of Irish history for all time.

That nurse's task had but begun: she was to risk her life many times trudging the wrecked corpse-strewn Dublin streets, amidst bullets and flames, with that fluttering flag of surrender. Dublin's history will recall with pride the names of many heroic women who risked their lives for freedom's cause, but this gallant nurse will rank amongst the greatest. To the day of her death—41 years later—she remained as loyal to her principles as that evening when the Commander-in-Chief of the Forces of the Irish Republic clasped her hand in final farewell at the Moore Street barricades. I was honoured to be her friend for many years—I did not realise the greatness of that honour. She was one of the rank and file who sought not place nor pay. The hall-door of her home in Lower Mount Street still bears her original simple name plate "Nurse O'Farrell" and is now occupied solely by her life-long friend—the last of that undaunted trio of women to leave the GPO in that Easter Week.

The nurse's first mission was to return with the Order of Surrender to No. 16 Moore Street, where she had previously been nursing the wounded, and now the final head-quarters of the Irish Republican Army, in the back room of a fish and poultry shop (Plunkett's), which the Volunteers had reached in their retreat from the blazing GPO after burrowing and hacking their way through the houses from No. 10.

It was evening before they vacated the battered houses, weary, hungry, sleepless, some with tear-stained eyes, and placed their wounded on stretchers and filed into the middle of the street; around them on the pavements and in the gutters lay dead soldiers clad in green and khaki, mingled with civilians—three of whom clutched white flags in their dead hands. How many of the green clad soldiers were in that ill-fated O'Rahilly column, who had charged from the top of Henry Street down Moore Street defiantly following their leader. Of this thirty followers only nine escaped unhurt—all the victims of Sherwood Foresters behind that Britain Street barricade.

Now that exhausted army formed in fours, sloped arms, and flanked by two soldiers with white flags, paraded up Moore Street around Henry Place, past smouldering GPO, its blackening granite shell glaring at them like a huge skull. Its waving flag of victory had gone—it had toppled into the blazing fortress—around they marched under the domineering Nelson—already licked in flames, towards Upper O'Connell Street, then halted, and laid down their arms in surrender under the flickering shadows of the once stately Drogheda House of the Moore earls. Then they moved on to spend that bitter cold night on the skimpy green lawn in front of Dr Mosse's Lying-in Hospital, around which once parked the delicate colourful sedan chairs. Now it was surrounded by British soldiers, with fixed bayonets towards the 400 prisoners huddled on the damp ground.

Four of those weary marchers from Moore Street would never again walk down that busy marketing area. One, the white-haired Fenian who had spent 15 years in English convict jails—still undaunted. Peering through his misty glasses, on the far side of the street he could distinguish his wee Tobacco shop, where so much had been planned for this Rising. Then the delicate, exotic, mystical poet-son of a Papal Count, whose frail health had sent him in search of the Southern warm sun. Was he thinking of Saint Thomas Aquinas or Saint John of the Cross as he shivered in the frosty night air? Or of his beloved Grace—whom he would wed by jerky candlelight in a dreary jail—his bride, wife, and widow in the one day. Then the gay, tireless organiser, the polio-stricken cripple, in agonising pain after his weary march without his stick, perhaps thinking of his humble Kiltyclogher home in the shadows of purple Ben Bulben and silvery, shimmering Lough Gill. And then the shy retiring sculptor, whose delicate hands had chiselled the "Mater Dolorosa" for Westland Row Church, and the Calvary for City Quay Church—thinking perhaps of his brother and would they ever again join in the boyish laughter in Saint Enda's. In a few days time they would all face the firing-squad, and their battered bodies flung into the same lime-filled hole of a barrack yard—to become the most sacred spot in Ireland. The military were now removing the barricade from the corner of Britain Street and Moore Street. The fight was over—or had it but begun?

Was the ghost of Earl Henry Moore hovering in those midnight darting shadows? If so, he could see eight houses aflame in his once elegant Drogheda Street, over fifty in Henry Street, over thirty in Earl Street, almost a dozen in Moore Street, and all this had once been the peaceful Ash Park of the great Abbey of Saint Mary along by the swelling River Liffey.

To-day, should another ghostly figure stride down Moore Street—that of the haughty Yeats—he would gaze on one of his sensitive poems neatly framed at a lane corner. Would it cause him to frown, or give a wry smile, or a meaningless toss of that handsome head? It is in memory of that gallant soldier, who, in a dying hand, scrawled a farewell note to his wife in the half-shelter of a fish-monger's doorway, before his bullet-riddled body sprawled into his own blood on the splattered cobble-stones of the laneway.

> What remains to sing about
> But of the death he met
> Stretched under a doorway
> Somewhere off Henry Street:
> They that found him found upon
> The door above his head
> "Here died the O'Rahilly
> R.I.P." writ in blood.
> How goes the weather?"

2

Around Historic Naul

It is not my intention to embarrass the inhabitants of this little village by stating that its existence is unknown to so many Dublin citizens, but to emphasise the city folks' loss in not visiting such a charming spot within eighteen miles of their homes.

Like most Irish villages it is a quiet one. It is surrounded by high hills from which there are magnificent views—the summit of one is the highest in Leinster. It has boggy marshy land, and also the best pasture fields in Ireland—comparable to that of the "Golden Vale". It abounds in history: two thousand years before the dawn of Christianity, stately warriors bore their kings and queens in mournful procession to their last resting place on its misty hills overlooking Royal Tara. Here, tradition says, that our National Apostle trod, and blessed the surrounding land, to be followed in the next century by the saintly Canice bestowing his sacred treasure of Christianity, and raising blessed wells, which still bubble today, to overcome disease. Here numerous battles were fought between Celt, Norse and Dane, and heroic pike-men rose, and fell, in brutal combat. And here the humble peasants toiled and sweated on their hilly fields, and skilled trade and craftsmen combined to make their little village almost self-supporting—many of whom had never walked the Dublin streets.

In the old days the Naul was an important village as it was on the main Old Drogheda Road. The mail-coach starting point was at Church Street. The coach was drawn by four horses, and on top, which was called the "Cock Roost", was accommodation for the less important passengers. It proceeded through the densely forested country of Ballymun—which afforded ideal protection for the numerous highwaymen then active in the city surrounds. It passed the "Boot Inn" and then "The Forest Tavern" on the opposite side of the road. A few miles further on, the male passengers had to dismount and push, shove, and haul the coach over the watery valley of Knocksedan to reach "Aungier's Inn" which topped the steep hill, where they changed the horses. The Abbey audiences often heard of Knocksedan, but many assumed that it was an imaginary place created by Sean O'Casey in his *Shadow of a Gunman*, where Maguire went "to catch butterflies", but lost his life in an ambush. The coach circled around the "Sweep of Rathbeale" where in the surrounding fields of the 15th-century Rathbeale House, 7,000 of King James's men encamped on the night of the Battle of the Boyne. It went through Ballyboughill passing the old ruined church which once housed the sacred Staff of Saint Patrick. Before reaching "The Nag's Head" with its thatched forge of the Donnelly family, it passed in one of the fields on the opposite side, the blessed well of Saint Canice, which was a certain cure for sore throats and headaches, but now trodden into the weedy, muddy ground. More humpy hills had to be surmounted before it descended on the nestling Naul village amidst a sweeping chain of fields. Here at the Inn, where the horses were changed again, the Great Liberator dined during his Repeal Campaign. The remains of the Inn still stand beside Killian's licensed premises. The coach then climbed the present "back Drogheda Road", through Stedalt, the rear of Dardistown Castle, and on to Drogheda through Beamore. One quails to think what was the fare from Dublin to Drogheda, when we consider that it cost 3*s*. 4*d*. from Church Street to Ballymun—the average wage then being sixpence a day. In those days the village boasted of its own stone-masons, nail-makers, carpenters, tailors, tanners, bootmakers, a bakery at the top of the hill (of which a little remains), three flour mills in the valley, and the very busy forge by the babbling River Delvin which separates Dublin from Meath, and was the border line of ancient Fingal.

The word Naul simply means "The Cliff" or "Rock" taken from the Irish word "An Aill". The vowel of the "an" having been dropped and the "n" added to the noun. The name arises from the large cliff or rock on which the foundation of the once mighty Black Castle was built—of black stone, which overlooks the once beautiful valley of the Roche. Through this valley of the Roche runs the river Delvin, which worked the busy mills—now all in ruins with slight remains of their multiplicity of dams and races. In an 18th-century book it is referred to as "a romantic and beautiful glen with mighty rocks, caves and water-falls", there is also a reference to its "health-giving Spa of Chaly-beate"—since lost in the churned mud. James Joyce makes a reference to "The Naul" in his *Finnegans Wake*, and Dr Oliver St. John Gogarty has written a poem of 150 lines "To the Mill at the Naul", which was printed in the *Irish Times* of 21 July 1934:

> I call to mind, to bring me sleep
> That ruin on the naming Hill
> Of Naul, with ivy on the keep
> That looks down on a ruined Mill.

The ruins of the Black Castle, now almost smothered with creeping ivy, was built in the late 12th century by Richard Cruise, Lord of Naul Manor. It was then protected on its North and East sides by the sheer cliff, and on the West by mighty walls. As was the custom of the Anglo-Norman castles, it had its spacious "bawn" to shelter its cattle herd. When the Cruise family participated in the Rebellion of 1641, they were dispossessed of their Castle and lands. In 1649 the Castle was destroyed by Cromwell, when 40 of its defenders were put to the sword—the lone female escaping. Oliver Plunkett was a frequent visitor to the Castle, and it is assumed that he was arrested there. In State Papers we find a letter from the Earl of Ormond, then Viceroy of Ireland, to Sir Hans Hamilton "demanding the capture of the Primate as a matter of extraordinary service to the King and of great advantage to Ormond himself", and hinting that money will not be wanting to secure the success of the enterprise. Sir Hans now writes to Ormond: "four days ago I learned from a popish priest—who some days before had gotten an induction to a parish from him (the Primate) that he (the priest) had left him at a certain place within seven miles of Dublin and that he (the Primate) had cut off his beard and wore a light-coloured wig and went by a feigned name". Two days later, on 3 October 1679, he further writes:

> Since my last letter I met the priest I mentioned. He told me he is confident we would find him at a place he left him, at which is an ancient Lady's house—in a Castle—about a mile from the Naul—near or on the

road from the Naul to Dublin—but could not remember the lady's name. He told me that I must direct my letter to: "Mr. McLeady" near the Naul (for he goes by that name). It is possible he may still be there unless he has been alarmed from Dublin, but I have laid out all his haunts in the whole diocese. So I am confident he shall not come hither but your Grace shall have a good account of him.

Others say that he was arrested near Finglas on his way to Dublin. The price on his head was 40 crowns.

Nothing remains of the White Castle. On its site is now built the superior residential Naul Park. The Castle was built in the 13th century by a Richard Caddell whose descendants were evicted by Cromwell's general, De Fyne. Later with its surrounding lands it was released to Arthur Mervyn, who built the three mills referred to, between the years 1718–22, to cater for the extensive corn-growing in the area. It was completely demolished in 1787.

In the graveyard, which contains many ancient headstones, stand the walls of the old church, first mentioned in a deed executed in 1200 which refers to the "Church of Stephen Cruise" built on the site of an old Celtic church. Within its walls is an old stone cross reputed to be of the 7th century, also the neglected vault of the Hussey family with their coat of arms, and a memorial on the outer church wall: "Erected by Hon. Edward Hussey and his wife Lady Mabel (née Barnwall) for their posterity in the year of Our Lord God 1710."

The church was burned and desecrated in mid-June 1540. The chalice was held in Clonmethan Church, until it was closed a few years ago. The Protestant Archbishop, Dr Bulkeley, in his Government Return of 1630, states that "the Church is in complete ruins" and that "Cruise—a staunch Catholic—Mass is said in his, or Mr. Caddell's house" referring to the castles. Late in the following century, when religious freedom had been granted to the Naul area—due to the influence of liberal Protestant landlords—the Hussey family commenced to re-roof the church ruins, but two Lord Justices at Dublin Castle "objected against the erection at Naul of an illegal Mass house", hence the ruins to-day. Mass was then said on alternate Sundays at the Black or White Castle. Later the people travelled over the right-o-way through Westown and Cabin Hill to worship at Dunrae mass house on the slopes of Malahow Hill. The Revd N. Donnelly in his *Short Histories of Dublin Parishes* refers to a Revd Owen Smith, P.P. between 1680 and 1725, who was ordained at Ardpatrick by Dr Oliver Plunkett residing this time at "the Mass house at Malahow". At Lecklinstown, in a small paddock beside a little brook, is pointed out a spot called "The Holy Studs" or "The Holy Stones", where Mass was celebrated during the 17th century when the Penal Laws were intensified due to the Titus Oates plot.

Collier the Robber, who like Robin Hood robbed the rich and gave to the poor, and kept a little for himself, on several occasions attacked the Drogheda Coach in the Naul area. His hide-out was in a barn south of Flynn's public house, now occupied by Macken's shop. In the centre of the village is a Spanish chestnut tree—replacing a weeping willow erected over 100 years ago by Hants Woods of Whitestown. It was planted there for decorative purposes, but its shelter and surrounding stone steps provide an ideal platform for political meetings. Under its shade was a butcher's stall, and here in 1903 came Michael Ó Maoileáin to teach the Irish classes. He walked from Saint Margaret's to the Naul, the next day he went to Garristown, and then to Bellewstown to teach further classes. Sean O'Casey shared his tenement room at Mountjoy Square; one night it was raided by the "Black and Tans" and this incident is portrayed in his *Shadow of a Gunman* and the character of Seamus Sheils is based on Ó Maoileáin. I wonder did O'Casey know that the Naul was the stronghold of the O'Casey clan whose battlecry was "The O'Caseys of the Spear." When Ó Maoileáin came to the Naul he stopped overnight across the road with Paddy Wherity. Paddy is just more than the ordinary local historian. He has the most uncanny memory that I have encountered—recalling verbatim from books that he had read over 60 years ago. He contributes extensively to the local papers on forgotten historical records—without resorting to any book or notes. Recently, in his 83rd year, he made a recording of an hour's duration for the Folklore Commission, on the Naul area, without referring to any documents—a remarkable

achievement for one whose limited schooling was handi-
capped with an embarrassingly severe deafness. I am indebted
to him for the valuable material with which he supplied me,
so willingly, for this paper.

On the opposite side of the River Delvin may be observed
a moat capped with trees. It is called the Camp field, as it
was here, on 1 July 1690, there camped the advance body of
the Williamite army. In this field it is also reputed that in
1052 the last king of Bregia—Maol na mBo—defeated the
last of the Norsemen. A year before the battle of Clontarf
Brian Boru had burned the Naul village as it was then the
strongest holding of the Norsemen in Fingal.

Associated with the Roche is the famous '98 episode of
"The Stag of the Naul": The "United Men" had treated
with the utmost suspicion the strange "French fugitive" who
had come to work at nearby "Moorside" seeking protection
from the English law. He spoke with a French accent and
acted like a Frenchman, and they nicknamed him "vive la"
as he used that expression so frequently. Their suspicion was
further aroused when he was observed cautiously sneaking
out from the Balbriggan Military Barracks. A short while
afterwards, at dawn, he was noticed slinking over the fields
with his belongings in the direction of Balbriggan. Quickly
he was pursued by three of the locals, over the hedges,
across the Naul bridge, down through the Roche—scanning
its rocks, climbing its cliffs, wading through its river, plod-
ding its marshy banks, again through the fields, where he
was eventually captured in the Camp field. Enough evidence
was found on him to justify their suspicions that he was an
English spy—for which he forefeited his life. One of the
burial party took possession of the victim's buckskin breeches,
as they were better than the ones he was wearing. Later, with
two of his friends, they were tried for murder, on the evidence of the clothing, at Ballbriggan Courthouse. They were
defended and freed on the brilliant defence of the infamous
Leonard McNally. For years after the name of McNally was
held in the highest esteem in Fingal. Almost a century was to
pass before it was revealed that he had so callously betrayed
his fellow patriots.

The Roche, with its numerous caves and crannies, was
the ideal spot for Collier to hide his loot. Here, smugglers

came to hoard their ill-gotten goods. It offered to evil Shaun-
Kithogue (left-handed John) and his formidable coloured
wife perfect security from the eyes of the law. A few of the
locals can still point out the almost obscure entrance to the
Piper's Hole, where many years ago a venturesome musician
piped his way through its dark recess, and the plaintiff wail
could be heard echoing from under the roadway on the outskirts of the village. For years afterwards, when the old people
were nodding by their fireside during the long Winter's night,
they whispered of the shrill vibrating music they could recog-
nise in the outside mournful wind.

The ruins of Westown House can be approached from
several entrances from the village. In a book of the last century
it was referred to as "A respectable mansion of antiquated
character in a highly timbered demesne containing a Rath,
and commanding a magnificent view of the beautiful Roche
valley". The original was built in the 12th century by a Lord
Beaulie, and the last of the family died in 1598, having
changed their name to Bellew. A few years later his widow
married a Peter Hussey, who had the mansion rebuilt about
1630 and renamed the place from Snowtown to Westown.
After the insurrection of 1641, the Husseys received a major
portion of the Cruise confiscated lands, including the Black
Castle, from Cromwell. In 1750 the last of the Hussey family
died and the property passed to a cousin by the name of
Stronge, who was obliged to change his name to Hussey.
The name recalls the Phoenix Park assassinations, as an
Anthony Hussey was the first juror called on the Invincibles
trial of 1883 and was challenged by the solicitor of James
Carey, but later he served on the trial of "Skin the Goat",
and on the third trial of Tim Kelly. At the end of the 18th
century the family erected a Community Barn for their tenants
on a piece of land in front of the present Church. On Saturday
nights the barn was cleared out for Mass on the following
day. A small portion of it was utilised as a school, and Paddy
Wherity often heard his grandmother refer to her schooling
there. The Husseys gave the present site for the church, and
generously contributed to its erection. The once strictly
private Hussey pew-gallery is now occupied by the village
choir. At the end of the church was the farmers' gallery and
was the prerogative of the large land-owners. Overlooking

the high altar is a dazzling stained-glass window by the late Harry Clarke. The old Naul school was built in 1831, by A. S. Hussey, which catered for 30 pupils. He also contributed £5 yearly towards the teacher's salary. In 1920 I went with my grandmother to purchase raspberries in the Naul. It was famous for the growing of this fruit. Every little dwelling had its garden of raspberry canes. All the gossip was of Miss Hussey's "posh" wedding, with the choir singing and the red carpet leading out through the Naul church. It was the last big event of the family. Twilight was rapidly descending on Westown House. In the early 1930s the estate was taken over by the Land Commission and divided amongst the local small farmers. For some years the house was occupied by the Martin family, whose son Liam is now well-known for his brilliant sketches of Dublin. The Martins were noted for their hospitality, and the last years of Westown House welcomed a motley gathering of visitors, including that versatile Dubliner, Brendan Behan, whose antics added to the merriment in the decaying Big House.

The house is now roofless—the valuable lead long since having been removed, and the surrounding stately timber sold, but the massive gaping ruins and extensive out-houses still testify to its once greatness—as ghostly they arise in the swampy jungle of once ornamental shrubs and the shimmering lily-pond. Many are the spokish tales associated with the dwellings. Only last year three courageous Dublin students camped throughout the night within the eerie ruins in search of some occult experience—much to the amusement of the villagers. Apparently, the students' quest was not unrewarding, in spite of their amateur undeveloped psychic powers to more fully pierce beyond the supernatural veil. Later some of the local youths might have a more successful vigil.

On the lands of Thomas Connell in 1949, amongst the bushes, brambles, and rank grass of the Four Knocks, was discovered what was to astound the professors of the archeological world—four pre-historic tumuli. One of them was found to contain a chamber wider than that of the famous Newgrange. Within the passages and side-chambers were strange stone engravings and scribblings, including the outlines of a human face. Numerous human remains were found which would indicate that the chambers had been built at the beginning of the Bronze Age—about 4,000 years ago.

Nearby is Harbourstown, with its quaint turret planked on its grassy moat. It is called "Cadell's Folly" and was built by Richard Caddell in the 1800s—for what, it is difficult to understand. The inside stairs no longer remain which once led to the roof from which, it is said, that the gentleman, with the aid of a powerful telescope, could view the races at Bellewstown. Nothing remains of his spacious mansion which far eclipsed that of Westown. It is said to have contained 40 rooms, including a chapel, and that his carriage drove him straight through the building to his bedroom door. But then sometimes facts are exaggerated, with all good intentions.

To Naul came Luke Teeling to supervise the Ford-a-Fyne cotton mills, after his beautiful home at Church Hill, Lurgan, and his extensive bleach mills had been wrecked in broad daylight by a mob of Orangemen. The history of the family during the '98 period is a litany of persecutions. The *Gentlemen's Magazine* refers to the Teeling family as "the best horsemen and the most accomplished swordsmen in the Province". In 1790 he had given active support to the parliamentary candidature of the Hon. Robert Stewart, who stood in the interest of Reform and Catholic Emancipation. Being a Catholic, Teeling was defranchised, so spared neither money nor personal exertion in favour of one who so eloquently voiced his ideals. At 15 years of age, Stewart had ridden at the head of a company of youthful Volunteers in a Review at Belfast. Later he was to be a foundation member of the "Irish Volunteers". But the lives of the Teeling family in later years were to be darkened when he became Lord Castlereagh. Teeling represented Co. Antrim at the famous Catholic Convention in Dublin 1792, and his friend Theobald Wolfe Tone referred to him as "the man of the Convention". Teeling had never given any sympathy to the violence movements, but his activities for unity between Catholic and Protestant had brought him under the suspicion of the Government.

On the morning of 16 September 1796, whilst Teeling and his 18-year-old son, Charles Hamilton, were on their morning canter, they were approached by Lord Castlereagh, in his usual suave manner, who was accompanied by two soldiers. Teeling was horrified when Castlereagh announced that he was placing his son under arrest for high treason. The young Charles had also come under the suspicion of the Government in his efforts to establish peace between the Catholic "Defenders" and the Protestant "Peep-o-Day Boys". Charles later was escorted with the United Irishmen McCracken, Russell and Neilson to Dublin's Kilmainham Jail, and confined to two years brutal imprisonment without being brought to trial. Before his arrest he had been offered a commission in the army, which he declined stating that "he held opinions which would ill become an officer of the Crown." The Marquis of Hertford renewed the offer on his release from prison, but it was again refused. Shorlty after the arrest of Charles Hamilton Teeling their home was raided by Castlereagh and his minions. The 14-year-old son, John, in the presence of his horror-stricken mother, was demanded, with a pistol pressed against his throat, to assist the soldiers in the search of the house.

The eldest and favourite son of the family, Bartholomew, became a captain in the French army and accompanied General Humbert, as his aide-de-camp, who had presented him with one of his rings as a token of his confidence, on the ill-fated expedition of '98. After this defeat he was arrested, brought to Dublin and, on the morning of 4 September 1798, at the early age of 24, hanged as a traitor. His body, with that of Matthew Tone and two hundred others, were ruthlessly flung into a dung field at the rear of the barracks. Today, that sacred spot at Island Bridge is used as an army soccer pitch. "Bartle" was an intimate friend of Lord Edward Fitzgerald and was in love with his sister Lucy. Before his execution he smuggled his last letter to his mother, enclosing a ring, inscribed "Erin go Brath" which had been given to him by Lucy, writing: "It is the dearest pledge of Love that I can leave you." More than eighty years after, the romantic token was presented by his grand-nephew—another Captain Bartle Teeling—as an engagement ring to his future bride. In 1867 he had been honoured by Pope Pius IX with the Cross "Fidi et Virtuti" in recognition of his valour in the pontifical campaign of that year.

Luke Teeling himself was arrested in Dublin in 1798, whilst waiting in Church Street for the Naul coach. He was imprisoned for four years—even though no charge was brought against him. Whilst confined on the tender *Postle-wait* in Belfast Lough he heard of the execution of Bartle. Later he was transferred to Carrickfergus Castle. The hardships he describes whilst imprisoned make pitiful reading. He was offered the advantage of subscribing to the Banishment Bill, to which he replied: "Mr Teeling, having never offended himself the laws of his country, nor given any cause for the outrages committed on his family, his property, and his person, cannot accept General Nugent's proposal of transportation nor any other terms that imply guilt." On liberation he returned with his wife to his son, Charles, then living at the Naul. On 15 October of the following year, his son Charles Hamilton was again arrested at his Naul home. Whilst in prison, the same bribe was offered him of an army commission by Colonel Campbell, and again refused. On returning to the Naul, he was to find that 25 acres of his land had been confiscated.

To the Teeling Naul home there came in the summer of 1799, with the intention of establishing a bleach mill for the manufacturing of linen, Jemmy Hope, that Northern Presbyterian United Irishman, who was the human dynamo of two Rebellions. For almost three years he remained with the Teelings, until he was spied upon by one of the employees—John Caroll—when he returned to the Coombe, where at No. 8, with the financial assistance of Teeling, he started a small haberdasher's store, directly opposite the temporary military barracks. Later he was to return to the Teeling home, with Samuel Neilson, during his secret visit to Ireland. Seamus G. O'Kelly in his book, *Sweethearts of the Irish Rebels*, tells us that Luke Teeling died during the Summer of 1822 at his son's Naul home, and whilst he as being waked a letter was delivered to his wife (Mary Taffee) informing her that their son George had died in Mississippi, and enclosed was the ring which General Hoche had presented to his brother Bartholemew.

To Charles Hamilton Teeling we are indebted for the intimate details of '98 in his masterly book, *The History of the Irish Rebellion of 1798*. When a second edition was called for, it was not forthcoming, and it was said that the Government gave the publisher a bribe of £10,000 not to republish it. Some fifty years later a Prime Minister of England, in a speech in the House of Commons, said that he "had no hesitation in saying that Charles Hamilton Teeling's *Personal Narrative of 1798* was one of the very best pieces of history extant".

About twelve years ago the Teeling Cotton Factory at the Ford-a-Fyne had to be demolished as it had become a dangerous ruin. However, it is regrettable that in the 1960s the historic home of the Teelings was wantonly destroyed, and its stones used for road-making—another of our historic legacies fallen a victim of commercial vandalism. Numerous papers of the Teeling family, including a fifteen-page report of the arrest by the local captain of the Yeomanry, of Charles Teeling, are somewhere in Ethiopia. Let us hope that they shall not be lost to our Nation.

Amongst the records of the Irish Sisters of Charity we find an Alicia Walsh born in the Naul on 25 June 1773. Today her name is linked with that of Mother Mary Aikenhead as the two founders of that great Order of Nuns. She was 39 years of age when they both set out to York to commence their novitiate. They established the first convent at North William Street, Dublin, and on the morning of 10 September 1816 they both commenced on the work of visiting the sick in their homes: "The first time that religious were engaged in such work". Alicia Walsh, now Sister Catherine, was to dedicate the rest of her life in the relief of the sick, the poor, and the imprisoned. At the request of the Governor of Kilmainham—a non-Catholic—they visited that prison regularly. During the dreadful outbreak of cholera in Dublin in 1832 Sister Catherine was continually in the shadow of death, constantly attending to the stricken poor at the temporary hospital at Grangegorman. She was a cousin of the Teelings, and her father though not associated with the activities of 1798 had his Naul property destroyed by the Yeomanry. Her relations suffered deeply, not only confiscation and oppression, but also the most barbarous tortures. She went from prison to prison to comfort them in distress, and several times visited Luke Teeling at Carrickfergus. In one of his letters he refers to "Ally Walsh, an uncommonly fine girl". Mother Aikenhead's father was a sincere friend of Lord Edward Fitzgerald, and undoubtedly because of these nuns' devotion to the national cause Lady

Lucy Fitzgerald, on her death, bequeathed a generous legacy to their Order.

In a field overlooking Loughmaine, at the top of Naul Hill, was the drilling spot for "The Defenders" under their captain, John Corbally, who was a tailor in the village. It was in close proximity to the Lecklinstown British Military Camp. Sir Rowan Hamilton in his memoirs pays a glowing tribute to Corbally, who later had been apprehended on a warrant for high treason. At that time there was a reward of £1,000 "to any person or persons who shall discover or apprehend the said Archibald Hamilton Rowan". The captain was offered substantial bribes and his freedom if he would inform on Rowan, but he refused. After five months' imprisonment the captain was transferred to Botany Bay and, whilst on the ship, was falsely accused of encouraging mutiny. He was punished by being put in chains and handcuffed to a corpse that had been flogged to death. Three days later he was de-chained as the putrified carcass had to be thrown overboard. Later he returned to England on a South Sea Whaler, and then to Ireland, where he died at his widowed mother's home in Naul. In the churchyard is a tombstone to the Corbally family dated 1859—probably this is his last resting place.

Thomas Pakenham in his detailed book of '98, *The Year of Liberty*, is of the opinion that the Naul played but an insignificant part in the Insurrection, and states: "At the Naul, in Co. Dublin, where the crescent shaped attack was to have had its Northernmost Camp—the insurgents had proved nothing more than a marauding band." This sounds incredible in view of Sister Catherine's statements, and we know that at this time a farmer by the name of Tiernan was a leader of the Insurgents and resided at the Ford-a-Fyne. It was over the shoulder of the Ford-a-Fyne hill, and past the Teeling Cotton Mills, that the harassed, fatigued column of Wexford insurgents straggled on their way for safety, to be finally slaughtered by the Dumfries Light Dragoons at Ballyboughill. Amongst State Papers in Dublin is a letter from a local captain of the Yeomanry, dated 30 October 1798, addressed to Edward Cooke, Esq., Dublin Castle, appertaining to the Ballyboughill last stand:

Sir, I was creditably informed that a Wexford man which had been wounded in the leg at Ballyboughill on 14th July last remained in the County and that he headed a party of robbers and was endeavouring to disturb the neighbourhood. I therefore took a party out some nights since and apprehended him in a house near the Bog of the Ring—in a retired place some fields from the road. He acknowledged that he came lately from Wexford. On examining him he appeared to have been wounded in the leg. From information I received I believe he was one of the rebels we engaged at Ballyboughill on the 14th July, calls himself Edward O'Neill, Coogan, or Hogan. He did not work or follow any honest means of livelihood and being a stranger should not be suffered to remain here. Notwithstanding the many robberies committed in this neighbourhood no farmer will venture to prosecute. Captain Bullock of the Dumfries—who commands here—has ordered a party to escort this man to prison tomorrow. Perhaps some Wexford men might know of his having been guilty and having fled to conceal himself—for he appears to be a desperate wicked fellow. I should not trouble you only it appears to me very important, for the peace of the neighbourhood, that he should not be let loose here.

I am, Sir, Your most humble servant. A gentleman told Alderman Lynham that he would supply evidence from Wexford to hang this fellow.

We now find another extraordinary document amongst the State Papers. Signed by the same captain and dated 9 November 1803. It is a poem of 40 lines dedicated to Bartholomew Teeling, and prefaced as follows:

Lines to the memory of B.T., a native of Lisburn, in the North of Ireland, who attempted to free his country from the merciless grasp of the foreigners, was taken prisoner and in the vigour of his youth publicly executed. O! Men of Ireland! remember that he who is tamely a slave offends his God and proves a traitor to the human race. The heroic fortitude with which he met his fate, the exalted qualities of his head and heart,

and the great and glorious cause to which he fell a mar-
tyr shall embalm his memory, and hand it down sweet
and pleasant to the myriads yet unborn.

The poem and preface are in a different writing from that
of the captain's signature. Are we right in assuming that this
had been copied from an original and submitted by the captain to Dublin Castle as evidence against the composer?

Paddy Wherity's grandmother was regarded as the local
"cure-all". From herbs that she gathered she could cure a
disease called "The Felon", also "The Wildfire" and ulcers.
From an ointment she prepared she could cure "The Blast"
in man or beast. Glancing through the Dublin Folklore
Records, it is stated that a Billy Barnes, or Barlow, residing in
the Bog of the Ring, many years ago, had the cure for cancer.
Mrs Colgan of Naul Hill cured ringworm with an ointment
made of May butter and sulphur and Hugh Gilsenan cured
the same complaint with a blessed cream and burnt straw
mixed in his spittle. Some women cured it with their wedding
ring whilst repeating a special prayer. When attacked by a
severe bleeding of the nose which could not be stopped by
the application of red flannel dipped in cold water and applied
to the pit of the stomach, they went to Mrs Marmion at the
Nag's head, who had her own cure which had been in the
family for generations. The quaintest cure of all is that told
to me by Willie Gilsenan of Kitchenstown, who as a child
had a severe dose of the whooping-cough. He was brought
out to the yard and three times rolled over and under the
back and stomach of a neighbour's donkey, after which the
animal was given bread to eat, the crumbs of which were
caught and boiled in milk which Willie drank. He is now 84,
and as he says himself "it did not kill him". His cosy home
lies at the foot of Knock Breac, where for several generations
the family were carpenter craftsmen: the business is now
extinct. Recently it took two lorries to remove their valuable
antique tools and farming implements to the Dublin Museum.
As a child, I remember Willie thrashing with his home-made
flail the wheat scattered on the barn stone floor.

Knock Breac is said to be the highest hill in Leinster: on a
clear day from its summit can be seen the Mourne Mountains.
It is now many years since the local athletes took part in the

Knock Breac Sports. In June of 1882 the gathering was entertained by the Forest-Boot Fife and Drum Band, and the music of the neighbouring Balbriggan Brass Band. One spring night a neighbour came rushing into the Gilsenan home, in an excited state, for them to come out and "see the little people running up and down the side of Knock Breac!" To his disappointment, they had to admit that they were denied a sight of his fairyland—and he was not drunk. No longer in the harvest moonlight do the wee green-clad fairy men, in their tiny red hats go riding on their prancing white horses around the lone hawthorn tree, nor Will-o-the-Wisp go hopping with his flickering lantern through the yellow furze bushes. And the farmer, ploughing its fertile summit for the Autumn corn, no longer treats with superstitious awe the three fairy mounds, but cautiously avoids disturbing that hallowed clay.

Now, we have all heard of Mother Goose, and of the Goose that laid the golden eggs, but few of us have heard of the famous Naul goose. She was simply called "Goosie" and died last year at the advanced age of 39. Laurence Flynn of Cabin Hill, who reared her from the time she picked her way from her oval shell to outer space, says that she was "the oldest goose in the world", and far be it from me to contradict a real farmer. Goosie was a most moral female and to the end of her days remained a celibate. She'd have no "hanky-panky" with her "boy-friends". The only time that she was introduced to the neighbour gander—two miles away—she looked around her and, raising her head, eyed him in disdain, flapped her wings, and took to the air, as awkward as a helicopter, and flew all the way home, astounding Mr Flynn that a farmyard goose was capable of such a feat—in fact he was unaware that a domestic goose could fly at all. Even Goosie was a bit of a puritan, she did not lack the maternal instinct; she was a doting mother and reared, after hatching, many a neighbours' sturdy goslings. Before Goosie was hatched, there resided on her road a tailoress whose skill was of more than local repute. Mrs Clinch was an invalid, and permanently confined to her bed. To use the old expression, she was "bed-ridden". Her nimble fingers could compete against any sewing machine for delicate intricate designs: her calico and flannel shirts were always the height of fashion for the farmers of the locality. My uncle recalls that it is nearly eighty years ago since his mother brought him to Mrs Clinch for his First Holy Communion suit, and how he screamed and yelled and bawled when they hoisted him into her bed to be measured.

On the night of 11 August 1881 there was great excitement in the Naul. Tar barrels blazed, the houses were gaily decorated, the Balbriggan Brass Band also blazed, and across the road spanned a banner of "Welcome". Hundreds surged around the platform under the Weeping Willow tree and cheered the three members of the Land League who had been released from Kilmainham Prison after their Holdings had been sold for non-payment of rent. John Gartland was chairman, and their president, Daniel Macken, addressed the throng. Three months later Macken would be arrested and sent to Dundalk jail. During that month of November there would be nine attempted evictions to be defied by the gallant women of Naul Land League.

The year 1921 the event of the "Fingal Bus". It passed through the Naul on its circuitous route from Garristown to the city. It was an event of major importance as no longer had the villagers to drive their pony and traps to Balbriggan for the Dublin train. It was a half-breed of an automobile—a cross between a bus and a charabanc. At first it was treated with the utmost suspicion and curiosity—and a danger to the community. Eventually, it was lovingly smiled upon and treated with that respect affectionately bestowed on their farm animals. It was sadly referred to as "the poor bus", as it puffed, moaned, and groaned, staggering up the steep hill— like a weary cow heavy in calf. To-day the CIE bus still only passes through the village twice a week, and often I have to walk the four miles to my grandmother's home, as my mother did seventy years ago.

One shudders to think how long such charming villages, like Naul, dotted over the immediate surrounds of our city, can manage to survive. Ambitious commercial combines are stretching their clawing paws to grab any green field that will further swell their already bulging financial banking accounts. Avaricious eyes are already cunningly focussed on the fertile land of Ballyboughill, in hopes of building what they call a "satellite garden town to accommodate 12,000 people".

Four miles further, in the dreamy valley of the Naul Roche, plans are being connived to build a four-acre sewage works. In a few years time, not Cathleen Ni Houlihan, but the citizens of Dublin, will be weeping for their "beautiful green fields" of Fingal.

I will conclude by quoting a few stanzas from a ballad entitled "The Muster of Fingal 1788", which was published in Arthur Griffith's *United Irishman* (the composer's name is forgotten). I found it reprinted in an excellent article on '98, by that Fingallian historian, Patrick Archer, in *Béaloideas* of Christmas 1939:

> The men who lived by Sword's old Tower
> Rose out in Freedom's morning hour
> While Lusk swift marshalled all its power,
> And did Corduff and Naul,
> From high Knockbrack and Mullaghoo,
> From Ballyboughill and Skiddoo,
> From Baldwinstown and Grallagh too,
> Came forth thy sons, Fingall.

3

Around Dominick Street

By the middle of the 18th century, Dublin, although only one-fifth the size of London, was then the second city in British Dominions. Its population had doubled since the turn of the century. The English Protestant gentry were beginning to regard the country as more than their second home, but one of permanency. The city with its puppet Parliament was really developing to the status of a capital. However, its centre was becoming unhealthily congested, the large timber houses falling into decay, the narrow streets—many of them only narrow bumpy laneways— were unable to cater for the huge coaches and the massive gilt carriages. Its general shabbiness and over-crowding was an embarrassment to the gentry and the new advancing wealthy merchants. To meet their demands for more commodious dwellings, new wider streets were developing on the fringe of the city.

Luke Gardiner—a wealthy retired banker—had already commenced building in patches on his land from the main artery of Capel Street towards Drumcondra Lane, and when he would have Henrietta Street completed it would be the broadest and most select in the city. However, almost adjoining it was a parcel of land in the possession of Sir Christopher Dominick, who would start building there in 1720. In 1727 a lease was made out for a house to Lady Alice Hine at the east corner and the lot is described as 'bounded on the north by the house of Sir Christopher Dominick". From this gentleman the street would derive its name.

Sir Christopher, it would appear, was a very devout follower of the Established Church, as in his will he emphasises "that any bequest to his wife or family be revoked if she allows any of their children to be carried to any Presbyterian Church, Meeting, or Assembly". When he died, in 1743, the bulk of his property with "three of his largest Silver Goblet Cups" passed to his son of the same name, later the property would descend to his sole grand-daughter—Emily Olivia, who would marry the second Duke of Leinster. Their new home further down the street would be their city residence until the erection of the present flats.

For over a century these lordly houses would be dazzling homes of an aristocracy whose extravagance would amount to a species of madness. Eventually their splendour would sink to the meanest of the Dublin slums—their snobbish owners forgotten, like the starving paupers who would die huddled in the bug-ridden, rat-infested basements of what had once been the crammed wine cellars.

The most important of the houses in the street is No. 20. It is almost a miracle how it has retained its former beauty with so many tenants with the passing of the years. Its interior is regarded as the most magnificent in Dublin. The plaster work of the ceiling over the spacious cum-staircase hallway is spellbinding, comprising of sylph-like maidens surrounded by birds, flowers, fruit and musical instruments, some of the figures extending over twelve inches from the surface. Robert West, who previously resided at Moore Street and was the outstanding stuccodore of his age, designed and built the house to his own specification, hence its unrivalled beauty. Later it passed into the hands of Rt. Hon. John Beresford, who was nicknamed "the uncrowned King of Ireland" as he boasted "that no Lord Lieutenant could exist in Ireland without his support". No matter how he may be maligned for his religious bigotry and opposition to parliamentary reform, and particularly for his cruelty to the '98 Croppies, he must be credited with the influence that he brought to bear on the Wide Street Commissioners of 1757. He was instrumental in procuring the services of James Gandon to undertake the building of our great gem of architecture, the Custom House. He persuaded Gandon to turn down an offer from Katherine the Great to build her a palace at Saint Petersburg. Probably at No. 20 he and Gandon discussed the plans for the future gems of our city, the Four Courts and the King's Inns.

No. 20 in 1856 was purchased for use as a Protestant school for the Parish of Saint Mary and remained so for 70 years. One of its teachers was Sean O'Casey's sister, Isabella, and from her he received his infant lessons before she was married from the house in 1889. Sean resided here for some time, with his mother, in the caretaker's quarters after his father's death, in 1887, when he was but seven years old.

The Parish was then a wealthy and large one, even though on the decline. Saint Mary's graveyard, now a public park, with its headstones planked against the walls, was then so overcrowded, we are told, that "in order to make room for others, bodies were taken up in absolute state of putrefaction, to the great and very dangerous annoyance of the vicinity".

In 1927 the house was purchased by the Dominicans as an Orphanage, catering for 30 to 40 boys between the ages of seven and fourteen. Their original Penal Day Orphanage had been in disused stables in Chapel Lane, off Parnell Street, which catered for twenty-five forsaken orphans. As a child I attended Miss Carney's famous concerts, which she held annually at the Foresters' Hall to raise funds for the Orphanage. For one penny we were allowed in to the dress rehearsal. It was an afternoon of pandemonium as not a word could be heard from the stage, as we utilised the auditorium as a playground. This is the oldest orphanage in our city, but no longer does it cater for scared children with shaven heads clad only in unshapely uniforms and noisy hobnailed boots. This once palatial house is now set out in dainty flats for youths facing the rigours of a commercial world.

Almost opposite to No. 20 was another Protestant school, No. 43, which little Johnny Cassidy was later to attend. At this school, through O'Casey autobiographies, we meet the Revd T.C. Hunter, who insisted on the half-blind child attending school and Church against the doctor's orders. O'Casey refers to him as "The black whiskered smug souled golly-wogged gospel cook, who brightened up the Will of God with his own", here were the children that called him "scabby eyes" and "the sour-faced skinny Miss Valentine", who treated him in scorn as she made his "chew chunks of the bible". Here he was brutally caned by the "scowl-faced, pink, baldy, hoary ould-headed teacher, Slogan". His brief and unhappy sojourn here was enough to deny him even the basis of a formal education.

As children, when we were leaving the Convent School, we used to shout at the Protestant lads, in our childish ignorance:

> Proddie Woodie on the Wall
> A half a loaf will do you all.

and how they gleefully retorted:

> Kattie Atie, going to Mass
> Riding on the Devil's Ass.

A few doors up, at No. 41, was the Convent of the Holy Faith. Up to 1800 it had been the town residence of the Earl of Howth, a Saint Laurence, who boasted that he was a direct descendant of Tristam, who gained the great victory over the Danes at Howth on the feast of Saint Laurence. He handed the house over to the Carmelite friars of Whitefriar Street, and in 1902 it was transferred to the Sisters of the Holy Faith, who moved up from their smaller school No. 54. Later they purchased the two adjoining houses: No. 39, the Western Hotel, and No. 40, once the residence of Sir William Fownes. Its narrow windows at the side of the door, topped with swags of flowers, are of special interest.

As a little chappie of five years, I toddled, in 1915, into the immense hallway of this huge building, clad in a blue linen pinafore, decked in a sailor's golden-lettered hat, with red, white and blue ribbons fluttering behind the rim, nervously grasping my Aunt's hand. It was my first day to attend school, hence I was allowed to avail of the respectable entrance. As my tiny buckled shoes clattered on the black and white shiny tiled floor I felt so dwarfed by the immense spiral staircase winding towards the white decorated ceiling. The lanky grandmother clock, in the corner, with its faded yellowish face resembled a nasty bogey man, and, in the alcove, the smiling Virgin with extended hands even appeared to over-cast the portly nun who beamingly welcomed me as I gazed on her swaying black crucifix in front of her stiff starched guimp.

Upstairs was the high ceilinged boys' classroom—which once had been the glittering drawing room of Lady Clanrickard. I was put sitting beside a little fellow who wore a more colourful pinafore, who later I learned came from a draper's shop in Capel Street by the name of Lemass, originally they had been called "Hatters". Another little Capel Street boy near me was Dickie Lenehan, whose father had a hardware business there. Crudely scrawled on one of the desks was the name of another Capel Street boy—then studying to be an optician, but whose future would be on the stage: Jimmy O'Dea.

Many of us thought that the nuns with the male names were men. Our play yard at the back of the school had once been the emerald lawns and flower gardens of Lady Clanrickard, the entrance to which was under the present stone archway beside the Convent. At the end of the yard had once stood the extensive coach house and stables, now replaced by the girls' school, where at Christmas was held the Drill Display and Concert. On the Sunday afternoon the nuns from the various convents came to the dress rehearsal, and when the curtain ascended we felt confronted by a colony of penguins. One of the little golden curled girls who sang with me in Cinderella—60 years ago—is still chirping and flittering around in the Rathmines and Rathgar productions. But the gay Prince Charming in her white wig and black velvet dress with its gleaming silver buttons who made my childish heart flutter with her winsome smile, was to meet a tragic end. The happy Madge, with her father, mother and brother would be battered to death in their home by German bombs on the North Strand during the War.

On Monday mornings, before rushing into school we gave a hurried glance across the street at the gathering of pale-faced women in their faded black-fringed shawls, clutching their bare-foot skinny children, in the shop's doorway under the three Brass Balls dangling pawnshops in our city, loaning pittances to the poor for their meagre personal belongings.

In two years' time the nuns will be leaving their historic Dominick Street Home. In these days of free education we are apt to forget how deeply we are indebted to this Order for their heroic work—in an age of pathetic religious animosity— to alleviate the poverty and ignorance of destitute children facing the horrors of the Victorian workhouse. The problems that then confronted them may no longer exist, but are probably replaced by more insidious ones.

A few doors up from the Holy Faith Convent at No. 38 a plaque was on the wall in memory of an extraordinary Irish child prodigy. We are told that when he was seven years old, he could read Hebrew. At twelve he was conversant with Latin, Greek and four other continental languages as well as Russian and Arabic. At fourteen he had the courage to write to the Persian ambassador in his own language. At Trinity College, in his 20s, he was appointed Professor of Astronomy and a few years later he was elected Astronomer Royal of Ireland. But to the world Sir Rowan Hamilton is known as a mathematical genius for his theory of Quarternions. The Hamilton family resided here until the beginning of the present century. Two of his daughters, Laetitia and Eva, became painters of note. All that remains of his house, in which he was born in 1805, is a blank plaqueless crumbling wall.

With the recent demolition of surrounding houses one can obtain a more detailed view of the beautiful Gothic Revival Church which was completed in 1861. It replaced several houses at the corner of Dorset and Dominick Street—including the one time palatial home of Sir Dominick himself, from which some of the hand-carved panelling had been retrieved and inserted in the new building. Much of the church's interior dignity has been affected by the removal of the delicately lace-carved Caen stone high altar, which slenderly tapered towards the richly decorated mosaic ceiling, backed by the multi-coloured stained-glass windows casting their mellow rays on the white edifice.

I was particularly saddened by the removal of the beautiful Saint Dominic's side altar, with its statues of the Virgin and Child bestowing on him the Rosary. When I saw them scattered in the back yard, I felt that the slaughtering Cromwell had returned on another plundering campaign.

On the gallery, behind the mighty thunderous organ, circled the stained-glass rose-tinted window adding beauty to the main entrance of the church. The seven niches over the doorway had once shadowed seven saints of the Dominican Order, but later they were the victims of a well-intentioned trial cleaning by a new apparatus of the Dorset Street Fire Brigade.

In my youthful days, the Church was famous for its numerous Sodalities. The Men's was founded in 1884 and boasted of a membership of 1,500, of which Matt Talbot was one. The whole Sunday Mass they sang in Latin. The Women's, which met on each Wednesday night, prided of a similar number. A one time President of it was a Moore Street business lady who owned a pork shop that was famous for its trotter oil. She looked an imposing figure as she glided down Moore Street on a Wednesday night, flanked on each side by her daughters who resembled ladies-in-waiting.

Of course I was a member of the Boys' Sodality, which was called the Temperance Sodality. Our final hymn was "Hail Glorious Saint Patrick", which was sung with a gusto that would shame a Hitler Rally, and when completed, Fr Costello would congratulate us on our fervour and admonish us to leave the church respectfully "like little gentlemen" and not disturb the slumbering nuns across the road in the convent. Our exit was boisterous enough to awaken the long slumbering souls in Saint Mary's churchyard beside the Liffey bank. Rushing by the Shrine of Saint Vincent Ferrer, we grabbed a few stumps of used candles to make a slide in the chapel yard. If stumps were not procurable, our religious conscience justified us taking a few new ones.

There were several attractive baits to encourage membership of the Boys' Sodality. There was the Annual excursion to some country beauty spot—ten trains were necessary to carry the contingent—much of the beauty had been tarnished by the time of our return. Eventually the word "temperance" was removed and we were just simply called "The Boys' Sodality". This became necessary as some of the senior members on one of our Outings to the peaceful bogside village of Moyvalley had somewhat disturbances to the respectable Kildare country folk. We had yearly sports in the Phoenix Park, and at Christmas took part in religious plays written by Fr M. Gaffney, who had dramatised the short stories of Pádraig Pearse and completed the unfinished novel by Canon Sheehan of "Tristram Lloyd", and who was later to embroil himself in an embarrassing controversy with Sean O'Casey about the rejection of *The Silver Tassie*.

The Imeldist Sodality was a gathering of young girls in memory of that remarkable child who, at seven years of age, had made such an impact on the Catholic Church that she was beatified in 1826. When I made my First Holy Communion I wore her medal surrounded in crinkled ribbon on my white armlet. At that time there was a little monthly booklet dedicated to her called *The Imeldist* which cost a halfpenny. It is now extinct. The centenary of her beatification, in 1926, brought a gathering of nineteen different nationalities to "Saint Saviour's". She is now vaguely remembered in a small stained glass window in the Church.

This was the first church in Dublin where the Rosary was recited weekly in Irish. The first recital was on 31 October 1898 and was attended by Michael Cusack, the founder of the G.A.A. On Easter Saturday morning of 1916 Pádraig Pearse attended Mass and Holy Communion in this church.

During the Forty Hours Adoration on 30 February 1921 the Church and buildings were surrounded by armed military, comprising of a dozen officers and eighty soldiers. Soldiers with fixed bayonets were positioned at the main entrance of the church and in the grounds. The search occupied one and a half hours when the sacristy and all living-rooms and bedrooms were thoroughly examined; however, nothing was removed, as we are told that the clergy were treated with much respect. The church and its congregation were in no way interfered with.

Frequently during "The Troubled Times" a shadowy figure could be noticed slithering through the presbytery entrance of the church in Dorset Street; he emerged out into the chapel yard, turned right down the lane way and disappeared through the back entrance of Vaughan's Hotel. It was the Irish Pimpernel—Michael Collins.

On Sunday, 7 June 1925, as Fr Gaffney was about to celebrate Mass, he turned to the congregation and requested them to pray for an unknown man "who had just died in the lane". When Mrs Keogh that morning was leaving her little shop in Granby Lane called "The Marine Stores"—which we school lads often "mosied" through, much to her annoyance—she noticed a man stumble and then fall on the opposite path. After going to his assistance, she returned with a cup of water and, as she pressed it to his quivering lips, he faintly tried to open his eyes, gasped, and sank back lifelessly on her shoulder. How in later years she would have been astounded to witness the pilgrims who would kneel in the dust and gutter, before the simple—almost crude shrine—that would be erected on the wall beside her humble home to the saintly Matt Talbot who had died in her arms.

In O'Casey's book *Innisfallen Fare Thee Well*, he would lambaste Matt Talbot with such thunderous blasts that he would dumb-found the enthusiastic devotees of their anticipated saint. The outspoken, somewhat bitter Sean also had that simple spiritual outlook, and when approached by

reporters towards his later days said "that he was busy talking to God". I presume that the simple Matt is now busy
chanting his hymns—which so much annoyed his "two-pair
back" neighbours in Rutland Street—before the Golden
Throne. And I like to think that he is accompanied by the
rousing Sean blowing his shrilling green bag pipes, marching
in his Saint Laurence O'Toole's kilt, displaying his knobbly
knees, both honouring the Divine Presence Who under-
stands our human frailties.

Dorset Street was originally called Drumcondra Lane,
and was called after Lionel Cranfield Sackville, who was
Lord Lieutenant for two terms, later becoming Lord Dorset.
A contemporary of his says "that he was of small ability, little
learning, but unscrupulously polished". He, and his son—who
had been dismissed from the British Army for cowardice—
had the reputation of the lowest morals in their society.
Drumcondra Lane at this time—about 1750—was the residence of several notabilities associated with the Smock Alley
Theatre. As the Lord Lieutenant frequented this theatre, the
street was called after him. Later he was to become the most
unpopular person in his circle through his introduction of a
Bill for paying a portion of the English National Debt from
the Irish Revenue.

Residing at Dorset Street was James Elrington, who for 20
years was the idol of the Irish stage, and we are told that
when he returned to Dublin after a year's stage success in
London, bonfires blazed at the street corners and the church
bells chimed to welcome him back.

But at No. 12 Dorset Street was born, on 7 July 1751, one
whose ability alone was sufficient to make our city famous.
The great Lord Byron in praising him said "that he has written the greatest comedy in English language, the best Opera,
the best farce, the best address, and delivered the best oration
ever spoken in England". Probably the happiest days of poor
Richard Brinsley Sheridan were when, with his father, he jostled down Dominick Street's cobbled stones, in their carriage,
to the Smock Alley Theatre. In 1816 he would die in London
in abject poverty where the sheriff had come to arrest the
dying man. Even when dead, attempts were made to seize his
body. A house in Dorset Street—now occupied by a window
cleaning company—bears a plaque as his birth place. But in

the *Irish Builder* of 15 October 1855, there is an article, and drawing of the courtyard of the proposed Dominican church about to be erected and it mentions that six houses, including that of Brinsley Sheridan, had been pulled down to make way for the foundation of the church which had been commenced the previous July. Let us hope that in his last dismal hours he was comforted by the memories of the heroic Anne Devlin, on whose behalf, in his prosperous days, he had sternly striven to have a parliamentary investigation into her brutal imprisonment.

Upper Dominick Street was not commenced until about ten years after the Act of Union—and on a much smaller scale than the lower end, where already the gentry were leaving to reside again in London to be closer to the parliament. Others were crossing the Liffey to the more select areas arising in that suburb.

In 1847 on the summit of the street was opened the Great Midland Railway, which was to replace the dreary canal fly boats, which had taken over twelve hours to reach Mullingar from the city. This was to bring immense changes to the area. The once wealthy big houses would descend to hotels, boarding schools, day schools and an influx of legal and business circles. A local paper of 1 November 1849 mentions that the Royal Albert Hotel has opened at No. 4 Lower Dominick Street where "its situation is central and in one of the most respectable and healthy streets in the City. Servants connected with the hotel are paid by the proprietors." The Howth Hotel at the corner of Old Dominick Street—even though it had been in business since 1820—announced "the addition of three suites of drawing rooms, has patent water-closets, stabling for fifty horses and most extensive coach-rooms."

Many quaint simple country folk must have passed, for the first time, under the lonely grandeur of the imitation Egyptian-Greek portal of the Broadstone. But undoubtedly the most pitiful of all that clattered down the Dominick Street pavements, in their heavy nailed boots, through the dull heavy city haze, were the rural labourers seeking a new existence in the already overcrowded city. The more ambitious ones gambled for a trifling better state of labouring in the English fields, or its smokey industrial towns. The even more adventurous ones seeking a better life in that New World across the extensive ocean. All of whom had hastily disposed of their small holdings for a few guineas—fleeing in desperation from their famine stricken surroundings around their dismal mud cabins with their crawling skeletons—the ditches choked with strenching bodies. All fleeing from stalking death to what they believed would give them a glimmer of new life. The Dominick Street down which they nervously descended, towards the busy city centre, was already being enmeshed by the gloomy shadows of decay and dark clouds of utter destitution. Its day of brilliance and grandeur was past.

In 1860 the City Fathers were contemplating that the circuitous route to the Broadstone should be made more direct to Henry Street, through Cole's Lane, by the removal of many corner houses. They considered that by the opening of this wider thoroughfare that a more modern market could be built and dispense with the unhygienic Moore Street and its surrounding filthy shambles. Over a hundred years would elapse before such an undertaking would be commenced.

Little did the humble parents of the little chiseller born to them on 31 March 1871 at No. 4 Dominick Street Upper realise that their future journalistic son—who would spend so much of his early life tearing down "the Paper Wall" that surrounded our country, would be the founder of a political party—that would exist even to the present day under different guises. Arthur Griffith—like so many of his youthful comrades who were prepared to sacrifice their youthful lives for their country's freedom—has been overshadowed by the vicious dark clouds of Civil Strife that cursed our country.

No. 11 was the residence of Sir Hercules Langrishe, to whom Henry Grattan paid the highest of tributes for his liberal ideas and for his masterful contributions to the Irish Parliament of which he was a member for 40 years. Sir Hercules, with Grattan, Lord Charlemont and Napper Tandy were the originators of the Volunteers. Alas, for all Sir Hercules' apparent patriotism, the secret Documents of Pitt reveal that he accepted £15,000 for surrendering his right to vote against the Act of Union. When he became Earl of Ely he moved to a more imposing mansion at Hume's Row—which was later renamed after him as Ely Place. After his death in

1810 his house was divided, and was later occupied by the Knights of Columbanus; one can still view its beautiful mantlepieces and ceilings.

Later, No. 11 Dominick Street was to be occupied by Mr William Walker, the city's Recorder. The sentence of horse-whipping for lawbreakers was then common. But his sentence was particularly harsh in the following case—the prisoner in question had been found guilty of stealing oats from a stable at the rear of a Dominick Street garden, which happened to be beside that of the Recorder's home, so the severity of the sentence can be somewhat understood. The verdict of his Lordship was that

> the accused be imprisoned for three calendar months, at the commencement of the term you are to be publicly whipped from one end of the lane to the other and back again, for I am determined to put a stop to oat stealing in this lane.

In 1831 the house became a boarding and day school whose principal, Dr Smyth announced that the curriculum included "Dancing, Fencing, Music, with parental solicitude in watching over the pupils' health and morals."

No. 1, the corner house at the east side of Parnell Street, which, as I have mentioned, was one of the first houses built in 1727 for Lady Alice Hine, was in 1794 occupied by Hamilton Rowan, the Secretary of the United Irishmen's Association. Already he had been imprisoned for his political activities, and it was from here that he escaped further arrest by lowering himself by rope from the back drawing-room window, and eventually escaping to France. Sarah Curran resided in this house with Mrs Hamilton Rowan for five months in 1803, when compelled to leave her father's home. It was not until November, nearly two months after his execution, that she heard of Robert Emmet being buried in Saint Michan's churchyard. She and Mrs. Hamilton visited the grave pointed out to them alongside the Church wall, and placed flowers on it, which they had purchased in Capel Street.

The wife of the curate of Saint Mary's Church, on the night of 28 August 1814, at No. 24 Dominick Street, presented to her husband a new son—Michael. Probably in this rambling house the slumbering babe had his first frightening dreams that were in later life to filter into his macabre stories of the Undead. The ghost stories of Sheridan Le Fanu hold a distinctive niche in English literature, and have been made into films. In 1840, when he was an active journalist he bought out three Dublin newspapers and by their amalgamation created our recently demised *Evening Mail*. His mother, who was the daughter of the rector of the parish, and cousin of Richard Brinsley Sheridan, was apparently a bit of a rebel in her youth, as she had the courage to steal Lord Edward Fitzgerald's dagger from the house of Major Sirr.

At No. 16 about the year 1766 resided the Rt Hon. Nicholas Loftus: the adjacent Loftus Lane was called after the family. If we are to judge from his will, he was a gentleman of great consideration, as in it he requests "to be buried at night time, without any ceremonies, assemblies, or mournings, but privately as soon as he was dead and desire that my wife and children wear no mournings". Regrettably, his wife pre-deceased him by eight months, but undoubtedly his eight sons and six daughters dutifully adhered to his request "and buried him darkly at the dead of night, by the struggling moonbeams misty light, and their lanterns dimly burning."

In an old paper of August 1782 we find that there was a Mr Westran residing at this number and that his house had been broken into by two boys of the names of Thomas Byrne and George Dalton, who stole a case of silver-mounted pistols and a silver Gorget. The boys also had in their possession a pet sparrow, and when the case was being held in court it transpired that when the youths were caught in the act of robbery the excuse they made for being in the house was that they were trying to catch their sparrow which had flown through the parlour window.

The house beside—No. 17—does not appear to be of any particular historical interest, but to me it is of sentimental value, as it was here in 1892 that two slips of country girls arrived on their bicycles to take up "rooms"—which we would now call a flat, as they were about to start their career in the Big City as apprentice dressmakers at Messrs Arnotts in Henry Street. Six years later one of them would marry the then only "purveyor" in Moore Street, and eventually I would be their "little gift from God". The two top rooms of the

house were then occupied by the housekeeper of the proprietors who originally had been the wet nurse to their children.

At No. 10 Dominick Street there resided in 1893 the Rt
Hon. Henry King who, I understand, was the second son of
the Earl of Kingston. In more recent years the Bourke family
carried out their business here as Theatrical Costumiers.
Here came Madame Markievicz and her husband to obtain
the costumes for their plays over at the Rotunda Concert
Rooms—now the Gate Theatre. Undoubtedly during her
visits Madame found time to drop in and have a hurried
chat with the mother of some of her Fianna Scouts who
lived a few doors up the street. Here at No. 10, what must
have disturbed the Spirit of the slumbering Earl as it echoed
through the lofty rooms of his once dignified mansion, were
the first strains of our National Anthem, composed by the
Bourkes' uncle, Peadar Kearney, and fingered out by Paddy
Heeney on his melodeon. We are indebted to the Bourke
family for the patriotic Irish melodramas which they produced at the Queen's Theatre during the height of British
hostilities in our city during 1917-21. The Bourkes, like our
National Anthem, still go marching on at their Dame Street
premises.

Some years prior to the Act of Union there resided at No.
57 one of the most trusted and respected of the United Irishmen. From a mere grocery shop in Mary's Lane he rose to
prominence at the English Bar. He was of a versatile nature:
an actor, a songwriter, editor of a paper, a dramatist—who
won the admiration of our Irish poet Thomas Moore. In a
book of celebrated authors published in 1788 his name is
grouped with that of Edmund Burke and the English poet
William Cowper. Later he was to acquire eminence at the
Irish Bar and become the intimate friend of John Philpot
Curran, and was respected by Theobald Wolfe Tone for his
national qualities.

His Dominick Street home became a nest of conspiracy
where he and his rebel friends conspired about the overthrow of the alien government. When the Revd William
Jackson arrived in Ireland on his mission from the French
Directory it was at this house that the French plans were discussed. When his national friends attended his suppers he
entertained them with his rebel ballads—his most popular

one being "the Lass from Richmond Hill". In later years he would eloquently defend the Sheares brothers, Dr Henry Jackson and Robert Emmet. It was only years after his death that his dreadful deceit would be revealed and his name for ever abhorred by all Irishmen—like that of Judas Iscariot. One of the jeering legal friends wrote a poem about him which contains the following lines:

> One leg is short which makes him lame,
> Therefore the legs do not tally,
> And now my friends to tell his name
> it is Leonard McNally.

Surprisingly, his name does not appear with his fellow informer, Francis Higgins, in letters of gold on the walls of the Rotunda Hospital for a £100 subscription to Dr Mosse's Lying-in Hospital. Apparently he had not the generous heart of Higgins.

A few doors up from the house of McNally, at No. 50, a new-born babe would draw its first breath on 21 February 1891. At the early age of twenty-five he would face the onslaught of an Empire's army with twenty of his Volunteers at the Mendicity Institute in 1916. A few days later the youthful Sean Heuston would splutter his life's blood on the Kilmainham cobblestones. More blood would be spilt before the sins of McNally would be obliterated.

The last house that I will deal with is that of the Duke of Leinster. This a a verbatim report sent to me by a lady who spent her childhood there with her father and mother who were the caretakers. It gives us an idea of the beauty and magnitude of these houses in the last century:

> The Duke of Leinster at 13 and 14 (including the Estate Office for Carton, Maynooth and other family castles) was the premier Duke of Ireland, head of the Fitzgeralds, of whom Lord Edward is known to us all. No. 13 was the residence, with lovely period furniture and a number of valuable pictures—original paintings by Old Masters in the drawing and dining rooms. The hall, floored with black and white large tiling, held a cosy covered "booth" for the hall porter. The roofs were provided with snow boards in winter. There was a

garden at back extending the width of both houses and down as far as the mews houses in Granby Lane. No. 13 mews was covered with an ornamental pear-tree; No. 14 with virginia creeper which also covered the boundary wall with the lane running from Dominick Street down to Granby Lane. 13-14 was a corner property. A gravel path ran down the garden; there were lawns on each side, with two raised, circular groups of ornamental shrubs. Right around the borders were flower beds. The Fitzgerald family, aunts, uncles, etc. of the Duke, all stayed at No. 13 when visiting or passing through Dublin. They were Lords—Frederick, Walter, George, were some, and the Ladies Alice, Mabel, Nesta. They were charming people; kind, interested in their employees and their families.

We now take a last glimpse of Dominick Street from its Parnell Street corner—where once stood the stately home of Lady Alice Hine. The gaunt, gaping, sordid tenements of my school days are gone—replaced by symmetrical, hygienic, comfortable flats, overlooking grassy patches with healthy leafy saplings. Behind, are the spacious playgrounds for the children—no longer barefooted, ill-fed or tattily dressed. But one can detect the creeping claw of vandalism, and wonders if Dominick Street will again descend to a dismal slum.

4

Rotunda Gardens and Buildings

If we had no Rotunda Gardens there would have been no Rotunda Hospital, and had it not been for the passionate humanity for the poor of Dublin of Dr Bartholomew Mosse, the son of a Maryboro' rector, born in the year 1712, there would have been neither.

He was 31 when he returned to Dublin from his extensive travels on the Continent, in his capacity as doctor with a licentiate in midwifery. His daily practice in the Dublin slums brought him in contact with the dreadful living conditions of the poor in the Coombe area. Their population was steadily increasing—under worsening conditions, "many", as he said, "living in cold garrets, open to every wind, or in deep cellars subject to floods from extensive rains". The streets were narrow and jumbled together, and into the yards was thrown from the windows the filth and refuse of the numerous families, which was seldom removed, and we are told, accumulated to the first floor windows. After heavy rains it flowed back into the hallways and cellars, as there were no sewers. The river Poddle frequently overflowed after such rains, thus flooding the low ground around the Coombe, and drownings of the unfortunate cellar-dwellers were frequent. Edmund Burke, writing from his home on Arran Quay in 1746, mentions:

> No one has seen such a flood as we have now—the Quay wall is scarcely discernible before our door. Our cellars are drowned, the water comes up to the first floor of the house, threatening us every minute with rising a great deal higher, the consequence of which would infallibly be the fall of the house. From the doors and windows we watch the rise and fall of the waters as carefully as the Egyptians do the Nile but for different reasons.

When the floods subsided, fever was the result, the poverty-stricken people lying on straw-strewn floors in their own rags and without any bedclothing. To add to the state of the over-crowding, beggars continually wandered into the city from the country—particularly during the Summer, demanding alms in a hostile manner, causing endless brawls and disturbance, and seeking sympathy with their act "roaring with hunger." Dean Swift called them "drunkards, heathens and whoremongers, and what they really wanted was ale, brandy, strong liquors and money, as they conceive that all this abounds in the city. In this town they have frequently been seen to pour off of their pitcher good broth that had been given to them, into the gutter. They should be horsewhipped out of the city." The vice of drinking was one of the greatest evils at this time, and it is said that ale-houses formed one-third of the total number of houses in Dublin.

Dublin at this time had but three hospitals, which accommodated only about 100 patients. The practice of midwifery was almost ignored—being in the careless hands of the apothecaries and surgeons. The College of Physicians had been granted a charter in 1692 giving them full power and authority "to examine all midwives, and to license and allow all such as they shall find skillful and fit to exercise that profession and to hinder all such as they shall find unskillful for practising." It is apparent that the College made little use of this charter, as previous to 1740 there appears to be only four such persons holding a licentiate for midwifery, only one being a woman. In 1753 the College declared "that a degree in Physics will be denied to any person who had done practice in Midwifery." So this profession was left in the hands of the unskilled to pick up their knowledge by practice on the poor, and there is plenty of evidence of their crass carelessness and ignorance in this direction. Certainly, Charles Dickens did not exaggerate when he wrote about Mrs Gamp and her companions.

Faced with these frightening conditions, Dr Mosse was determined that an effort must be made to build a hospital, and train a staff to save the hundreds of women who died in childbirth, as he said "with their infants the country was thus being robbed of mother and child." Like all men of vision he was faced with hostility when he should have been encouraged and he was jeered by his fellow doctors as being an unbalanced idealist. So, with his own money, the help of a

few sincere friends, and an abundance of courage, he opened
this humble hospital, which could cater for only ten patients,
on 15 March 1745—the first undertaking of its kind in the
British Dominions, and he stipulated: "Every woman to have
a decent warm bed to herself and to be provided with all
manner of necessities, and the greatest imaginable care will
be taken of her and her new-born infant from the time she is
admitted and until well able to leave the hospital, and all
without the least expense to her." It was situated in George's
Lane, now Great George's Street, and opposite Fade Street.
In 1908 it was pointed out as being Nos. 56 & 57. Originally
it had been run as a house of amusement by a famous Italian
pantomimist, Madam Violante, whose group of dancers,
swordsmen, jugglers and tumblers performed in the front
yard. Madam herself, we are told, who "was no longer young
and never beautiful, gave demonstrations of rope walking
showing her limbs which did not meet with the same success
in this Kingdom as she had found in England." Later she
changed over to plays and comic opera, her company including the future famous Peg Woffington. Eventually, the Lord
Mayor had Madam's premises closed down.

In the first year of the hospital only one of the 209 women
admitted, died, and 190 babies had been safely delivered.
That year applications had been made to him from London
for plans and details of his undertaking, and the following
year three such hospitals were in the course of construction
in that city. It was all so encouraging, but also so dishearten-
ing, as he could not cope with the growing number of applications for admission, but now that it was a success he had
numerous offers of help. So he was determined to procure a
larger building. With additional aid, the running of concerts
and large scale lotteries—we are told that he sold 1,000 tickets
each day at the hospital at half a guinea each, which were
then the rage—he was able in 1748 to procure the lease of an
ugly patch of marshy land of four acres plantation measure
which was surrounded by a few cabins. It was situated on a
hill known as the Barley Fields and then regarded as being in
the country. It was a memorable spot on which the Irish
inhabitants had overthrown the Danes. The city at that time
had scarcely extended beyond present Parnell Street; Dominick Street had but been opened up a few years previously to

Drumcondra Lane—later named Dorset Street, and few of
its palatial houses had been completed, which were eventually to decay into one of the worst slums in the city, now
nearly all replaced by hygienic flats. The present O'Connell
Street was but a narrow roadway with only a few houses and
called Drogheda Street. In 1758 it would be widened with
its beautiful mall and trees, and renamed Sackville Street.
His first move was to have the patch of ground surrounded
by a high wall and to have it fashioned on the style of the
then famous London Vauxhall Gardens so as to provide
funds for his hospital. Dainty gravelled paths were laid out
and surrounded by ornamental trees and shrubs and attractive flowerbeds. Miniature waterfalls and splashing fountains
were installed and numerous coloured lamps adorned the
walls. Then cosy coffee houses were erected and a concert
hall, and on top of the hill was perched a band terrace where
an orchestra, dressed in gaudy uniforms, performed popular
music of the day. An added attraction at the bottom of the
hill was the emerald green bowling pitch. Attractive concerts
of every description, at which the cream of talent contributed, were the delight of all. The New Gardens, as they
were called, became the rendezvous of the Lords, Ladies,
Dukes, Earls and Members of Parliament, whose style and
fashion vied with that of the Vice-Regal Lodge. Lord Clon-
curry had written that "Society in the upper class at that
time was as brilliant and polished as that of Paris in the best
days, while intercourse was conducted with a conviviality
that could not be equalled in France."

They were like a gay carnival throng that had whirlwinded
from a theatre rather than from the lordly mansions of the
town in their variety of costumes. The ladies in their dove-
coloured crinolines, or flowing rose-tinted skirts with their
pale satin shoes, ribbon streamed bonnets perched on their
wriggling curls, or perhaps hatless in their high freakish hair
do's, and they fingering their flimsy parasols or finely painted
ivory fans. By no means did the gentlemen lack colour. They
were dandies, in their powdered wigs, silk coats with huge
braided cuffs, white laced cravats, narrow embroidered
trousers, complete with patent shoes with large silver polished buckles, waving their gold topped black cane walking
sticks, re-inforced by the military in their blaze of colour

with their dangling sheathed swords. They were a social gathering and did not shrink from the admiring gaze or near contact of the less affluent public, who could satisfy their curiosity and stare on this motley swarm for the admission fee of five pence of the realm.

On one morning in each month the Doctor gave a gratis musical breakfast to entice new subscribers for his hospital. That delightful chatterbox friend of Dean Swift, Mrs Delaney, describes attending such a function. Writing from her Delville home in February 1750, she says:

> The music allured us and we went at about half an hour after eleven, the concert to begin at 12. When we came, with some difficulty we squeezed into the room and got up to the breakfast table which had been well pillaged, but the fragments of cake, bread and butter, the silver coffee pots and tea kettles without number, and all sorts of Spring flowers strewn on the table, showed it had been plentifully and elegantly set out. The company indeed looked as if the principal design of coming was for a breakfast. When they had satisfied their hunger the remains were taken away and such a torrent of a rude mob, for they deserved no better name, crowded in, that I and my company crowded out as fast as we could, glad that we escaped with whole skins, and resolving never more to add to the throng at gratis entertainments. We got away with all speed without hearing a note of music.

Money rolled in, and rolled out, from the lotteries and the Garden amusement for the George's Street Hospital, all of which were supervised and conducted by the Doctor himself, and then on the morning of 9 July 1751 was laid the foundation stone of the new hospital, by the Lord Mayor, which was but proper as it was intended for the destitute. After which the joyous Doctor entertained the distinguished to a genteel breakfast and suitable concert in the Gardens. On that evening he admitted to his friends that he was worth barely £500, although he knew that the hospital would cost £20,000 to complete.

Now jealous tongues began to wag: that the object of the undertaking was to make fame and fortune for himself under the cover of charity. To protect his honour, he had the original lease endorsed that "he did acknowledge and declare that the said lease and ground was taken by him in trust for and to further the use only on behalf and benefit of the Hospital for the distressed and poor lying-in women."

His unselfish work was being recognised. In 1756 he was granted a royal charter for the Hospital, and the Corporation and Government provided a reasonable amount of funds for the new building. The work was undertaken by the distinguished Richard Cassels, then at the height of his fame; already to his credit were Leinster House, Clanwilliam House, Tyrone House, and Carton House at Maynooth then being completed. He was a friend of the Doctor's and appreciated the sacrifices he had made for this charity, and it would appear that he undertook this work voluntarily. Unfortunately, he died before it was completed, and it was finished by John Ensor; on 8 December 1757 it was declared open by the Viceroy, the Duke of Bedford, accompanied by the Duchess, before a most distinguished gathering, supported by the dignitaries of Church and State, who chatted with 52 destitute expectant mothers who were being admitted to the wards that day.

The distinguished dome was then surmounted by a cradle in black and gold—a rather fitting trade mark—but it had to be removed twenty years later for safety purposes. Dr Mosse had expended £65 for a clock and chimes, but the dear ladies of the surrounding houses complained that it would disturb their sleep. So the considerate Doctor acquiesced. It had also been his intention to erect an observatory in the tower and had already provided the telescope, but this plan did not materialise.

Now he embarked on his sublime golden dream—the chapel. It was his intention that it be the most artistic of its size in Europe. Certainly there is nothing else like it in this country. It is the work of Barthélemy Carmillon, but it was all supervised by the Doctor, drawing on the artistic knowledge that he had acquired on his Continental travels. One gazes in wonderment, from the polished mahogany pews and similar panelled walls surmounted by the various coats of arms, at the delicate wrought-iron balcony and the ceiling of multi-coloured stucco work of perplexing allegorical

images. The mother with the suckling babe at her breast—
symbolising charity. The beauty of the work is intensified by
the simplicity of the altar between the Corinthian pillars of
black and gold, crowned by the Lamb of God lying on the
Sacred Book with its Seven Seals, all surrounded by winged
cherubs' heads, clustered vines and olive branches, scarlet
hanging festoons and puffy blue and white clouds. From the
centre of the ceiling suspends a brass 18th-century crystal
lantern. The centre piece Mosse had intended for a painting
of the Nativity and was in correspondence with the great Italian
artist Cipriani—then residing in London—about its details,
whom he cautions "that care must be taken with your brush
to keep clear of any Catholic reminiscences, as the Chapel is
intended only for Protestant worship." The pews were rented
out to the highest bidders, and the revenue received exceeded
the Governors' most sanguine expectations. For the year
ending December 1763 the pews brought in £80.15*s*. 3*d*.,
and the yearly weekly collections were £117.10*s*. A tidy sum
of money for that period. The Chapel's three windows look
onto the skimpy lawn in front of the main entrance to the
hospital, on which were huddled 400 Irish prisoners after the
surrender of the blazing GPO, on that bitter damp Easter
night 1916, surrounded by British soldiers with fixed bayonets.

Alas, the great Doctor did not live to see his dream chapel
a reality. His health became seriously impaired due to
intense study and application of mind, close attention to
business and supervision of the hospital, and the fatigue of
the frequent journeys to London in connection with the
Lotteries. He died in Ranelagh, at Cullenswood House on
16 February 1759. This house in September 1908 opened to
the merry laughter and boyish shouting of Padraig Pearse's
first Saint Enda's School. In the hall-way can still be seen
inscribed in ancient Irish the quotation of his hero, Cú Chu-
lainn: "I care not if I live but a day and a night if my fame
lives after me." What should be preserved as a shrine for the
Irish nation is now occupied by five families. It is amazing
that the papers gave scant reportage to Dr Mosse's death,
and the Hospital records contain no Resolution of sympathy
with his distressed wife. They were seventeen years married,
and she was left with two young children and in indifferent
circumstances. Some time later we find the Hospital Com-

mittee "ordering that she will quit the House by Michaelmas next." She died three years after him at Great Britain Street, and it is gratifying to know that Parliament had granted her £1,000 "in consideration of the merit of her late husband in regard to the poor." The Board had then decided that in future the Master must reside outside of the Buildings, but in 1773 this rule was rescinded, so the Master and family since live on the Hospital grounds. For nearly a hundred years, we are told, Dr Mosse's name was forgotten, until rescued by Sir William Wilde, the father of Oscar Wilde, in a lengthy memoir which he published in the *Dublin Quarterly Journal of Medicine* in 1846.

Perpetual Summer is the doubtful prerogative of few countries—certainly not of Ireland. So now the Governors embarked on the construction of a new building which would cater for the New Gardens' activities during the Winter and inclement weather. Certainly it would have been a sin against good taste not to avail of the fashionable overflow. So the new building was undertaken by Ensor and completed in 1767. It was called the Rotunda, which name would eventually be applied to the Hospital itself. It accommodated more than 2,000 persons, and had the advantage of requiring no central supports, had perfect acoustics, the most modern decorations, adorned with fluted Corinthian pilasters, high expansive windows, and its dazzling ceiling of white and gold dangled with crystal glass chandeliers flickering their white wax candles. It was to house the most elaborate and important functions of the country and bring much needed finance to the Hospital. Its balls, masquerades, oratorios, and classical concerts would indeed be added attractions for the avaricious pleasure-seeking society. The renting of the room for one night in 1768 was 60 guineas.

On 17 July 1785 the Duke of Rutland, then Lord Lieutenant of Ireland, laid the foundation stone of the further buildings attached to the Round Room, which were called the Assembly Rooms. Though on a smaller scale, they possessed all the grandeur of the Rotunda. Upstairs, which was called the Supper Room, had another beautiful ceiling with shining brass chandeliers with clear crystal droplets and panelled decorated walls. Its twenty tables catered for fifteen persons each, with a profusion of food, gleaming silver-ware and various coloured wines in cutglass decanters, each table decorated and set alike to avoid preference. Underneath was the spacious Pillar Room, then regarded as the best of its kind in the British Isles, and compared with the Ballroom at the Bath health resort. This also had a beautiful ceiling, marble pillars and gilded mirrored walls, adding sparkling reflections to the gliding dancers. It also had a variety of ante-rooms which provided cosy nooks and alcoves for the coffee-drinking gossips or the jolly players of cards. Now the buildings and gardens satisfied every curiosity that art could perceive, imagination suggest and vanity desire for the aristocrats of the new palatial houses that had sprung up around the Gardens. In 1792 it was the homes of eleven peers, a peeress, two bishops, and twelve members of Parliament, and over-aweing them all was the expansive Charlemont House. The Square even eclipsed the grandeur of Saint Stephen's Green and its fashionable Mall. In No. 10 resided Lord Longford. In a few years time his sister's sensational wedding to the famous Duke of Wellington would take place in the drawing-room. In later years one of the Longfords would become a Gaelic scholar and senator, a patron of the Arts, and would save the distinguished Gate Theatre, across the Road, in the Supper Room, founded by the dual genius Edwards-MacLiammóir. Outside, high on the front of this building, almost indiscernible in the grime-coated stone, is the crest of the Duke of Rutland, surrounded by crowns, harps, and shamrocks, after whom the Square was called in 1785. He was a generous friend of the Hospital, and his name and that of the Duchesss appear on the Benefactors' list displayed in the Hospital corridor, together with many others including the Duke of Leinster, the Guiness family, Sir Robert Peel, Henry Flood and Chester Beatty. A donation of £100 was received in 1804 from Francis Higgins— better known in Irish history as the Sham Squire. He then resided at Lower Dominick Street; the house has been demolished. Kind Edward, on his Dublin visit, graciously donated the sum of £2,500, but it was from a gift of £50,000 already subscribed for him by the loyal citizens of Dublin. His Royal Mother, on her visit in 1900, gave only £50, but, as there is no mention of her being the recipient of any royal gift, we must assume that her contribution came from her Post Office Account. So anyone now wishing to contribute the sum of £50 for the continued good work of Dr Mosse's Hospital can still have his name engraved in letters of gold amongst this list of famous and infamous benefactors.

In 1748 the high walls surrounding the Gardens were removed and replaced by the present dwarf ones and railings which were thickly set with lamps. These lights provided another source of revenue for the Hospital, as "the resident of the Square paid 1s.9d. per foot for the lights" and for the private lamps outside their own homes they contributed £1.14s.0d. per year. No house had less than two lamps, many had three, and Charlemont House boasted four. The smallest house paid £5 per year to the Hospital fund and Lord Charlemont paid £16.16s.0d. There is but trivial trace of these once helpful lights. The following year the Government granted the Hospital a further perquisite: a duty of £1.15s.0d. on each sedan chair privately owned. A fine gesture, when you consider that there were 260 such modes of conveyance in the city. No lady at that time would consider venturing out on foot. In fact, such a chair was indispensable to every city family of distinction, as well as a coach. We are told that Henry Grattan was brought in the early hours of the morning, to make his last speech in Parliament against the Union, in a sedan chair. Like the early days of the motorcar, they were more than a bit of a nuisance, as the Bearers were a troublesome lot—continually interfering with the rights of the citizens. They possessed formidable weapons in the poles of the chair, which they frequently withdrew for combat, and they violently resented the introduction of the umbrella as a danger to their profession. Disrespectfully they were called "men mules" and "christian ponies." This duty brought into the Hospital in 1787 the amount of £547. We learn from Watson's *Dublin Directory* of 1822 that a setdown within the public lights for a sedan chair was at that time 6½d., for the first hour 1s.1d., and for every half-hour afterwards 9d. After midnight the uniform charge was 1s.7½d. A sedan rank was at the corner of the Gardens nearly opposite Charlemont House, and also at the other corner opposite Findlater's Church. The pillared shelters were still there when I played as a child in the Gardens. They were also parked at the back of the Pillar Room in the Gardens, and between the Ambassador Cinema and the front entrance of the Hospital. To the patients it must have been a disturbing noise—the

shouting of the sedan carriers, the rumbling of the coach
wheels, the yelling of the link boys, and the spluttering of the
sparking flambeaus. It is just as well they were denied the tin-
gling of the dome's chiming bells.

The Rotunda Rooms were now called the "Forum of Ireland" and probably its most intoxicating gathering was that
which took place on 10 November 1783, when its massive
doors flung open to the booming of artillery, the music of
regimental bands, the roar of cannon fire and the rattle of
drums, to receive the delegates of 100,000 volunteers from
our four Provinces, headed by the Earl of Charlemont with
his scarlet-and-gold uniformed Guard of Honour, followed
by the guards of the Light Dragoons and Squadron of Horse.
Their meeting would last for three weeks and come down in
history as the "Rotunda Convention." Here, on 4 April 1792,
a little boy of eight years from Golden Lane delighted the
huge fashionable audience with his performance on the piano-
forte. He was really ten, but what a difference a few years
when the child was a prodigy. Little Johnny Field's nimble
fingers would waft him through the capitals of Europe to the
Royal Court of Russia to be honoured with the title of Chapel
Master of the Emperor of Russia. He would compose the
original nocturne which the great Chopin would imitate. A
beautiful memorial decorates his Moscow grave. He is still
honoured in Russian musical circles—mostly forgotten in his
own city.

For the three years after the outbreak of the 1798 Rebellion it was utilised as a military barracks for the sum of
£1,450 per annum. Later it would echo to the booming
oratory of the Great Liberator. From its stage the great
cardinals, Newman and Wiseman, would propound the philo-
sophies of their Church.

On the evening of 26 August 1858 thousands mobbed the
building, broke the pay-box windows, and offered £5 per
seat, clamouring to hear the readings of the famous Charles
Dickens. 3,000 people packed the room on the night of 23
October 1878, even though the admission fee was 6*d.*, to
shout and cheer their Chief, Charles Stewart Parnell.

During the week of 1 August 1910 the Round Room was
packed each night with Gaelic League activities, and at the
Ard Fheis elected to the Coiste Gnótha was the compara-

tively unknown Cathal Brugha, Pádraig Pearse, Seán T. O'Kelly and Thomas Ashe, and Dr Douglas Hyde presided. All would cast their shadows on the pages of Irish history. One evening there was discussed "That Faust should be translated into Irish." The speakers taking part were: Vincent O'Brien (was his pupil John there?), Alice Milligan, the Tyrone poetess, Seamus Clandillon (later the first Director of 2RN), and the blind Belfast composer Carl Hardebeck, presided over by that remarkable, and now forgotten man, Edward Martyn, who contributed so much of his wealth to the Irish cultural revival.

For the Horse Show week of that year was billed the "first exclusive showing in Europe—at enormous cost, the sensational Johnson and Jefferies World Championship film at Reno." There was to be a special screening of the film each morning at 10.30. It was to be the attraction of the year. But another sensation was to loom. His Grace, the Archbishop of Dublin, Most Reverend Dr Walsh, announced his protest to the Right Honourable Lord Mayor of Dublin:

19th August, 1910.

My dear Lord Mayor,

I saw with satisfaction that the London County Council recently expressed a strong opinion adverse to the exhibition of a cinematograph reproduction of the brutalising Johnson and Jefferies fight in America.

Now it appears that Dublin is to be made a sort of "jumping off" ground for the display. Cleverly enough the showmen have selected the Horse Show week for their performance here.

Those of us who know Dublin well know that the Horse Show, full of advantages as it is for so many interests, has its drawbacks, and amongst them one of a very demoralising kind.

Things being as they are, the cinematograph display will be attended by a crowded audience. That, unfortunately, we cannot help. But we can at all events register a protest against it.

I remain, dear Lord Mayor,
Your Lordship's faithful servant,
Wm. J. Walsh.

However, the film went on as scheduled, for a week, to packed houses, the audience including many clergy.

At the back of the Pillar Room, extending into the Gardens had been erected a skating Rink, which was capable of holding between 5,000 and 6,000 people. On the night of 26 November 1913 an assembly of young men overflowed into the Gardens. The purpose of the meeting—to inaugurate the Irish Volunteers. When Eoin McNeill had finished his address to the huge assembly, he said: "We will start now, in the name of God." 4,000 Volunteers joined that night. After the burning of the GPO in 1916, the Rink was taken over by the Post Office and used as a sorting office. Some years later—during what is called the troubled times—it was completely burned down.

In the Pillar Room on 16 July 1927 was witnessed the most pathetic scene of all. It is estimated that 100,000 people throughout the day and night filed around the flag-draped coffin of her who had gaily waltzed at the Vice-Regal Lodge and curtseyed at the Whitehall Court before the regal Victoria—the beautiful Constance Georgina Gore-Booth—later to be the first woman elected to the British House of Commons. Now in that silent dim dance-hall with its pale flickering candle lights, guarded by her green uniformed Fianna Éireann Boy Scouts, brawny labourers and black-shawled street dealers, their ghostly figures starkly reflected in the mirrored walls, sobbed as they peered through the misty coffin glass panel on the contracted worn features of Madam, "the friend of the toiler and the lover of the poor".

In 1779 the then Master of the Hospital, Mr Frederick Jebb, had caused much alarm to the officials at Dublin Castle. He was of a patriotic nature and had written several articles of this kind for various newspapers which caused some disturbance at the Vice-Regal Lodge. However, it is apparent that he came to terms with the gentlemen in question, as the following is one of the letters written, the next year, by the Lord Lieutenant to the Government:

> Dr Jebb, who was the chief of the political writers, has agreed on the terms of my recommending him for a pension of £300 per annum to give his assistance to the Government. Since that time he has been very useful by

suppressing inflammatory publications by writing and other sources, which he promises to continue to the extent of his power.

One of the previous Masters, Dr William Collum, from 1766 to 1773 appears to have got into difficulties with the Governors for lack of attendance at the Hospital. It would appear that he was accused of paying too much attention to his own Private Nursing Home at 41 Moore Street. Apparently Moore Street was then a residential area, if we are to judge by the number of retired clergymen then residing in the street.

In 1816 the Hospital records show an unaccountable deficit of £1,530. An investigation was immediately demanded, and later we read in the Newspapers of the tragic suicide of the unfortunate Registrar.

1825 was a winter of extreme severity, and there occurred an incident over which the Hospital authorities had no control, but which must have caused them great anxiety. In one of the surrounding streets were found two dead women in the snow, with their new-born babies, who apparently were making their way to the Hospital for their confinement.

The history of the Hospital has been a continual uphill fight to produce the necessary finance for its upkeep, extensions and improvement. Over-crowding was a continual problem—as the Hospital had always boasted that a destitute expectant mother had never been turned from its doors. In its frantic appeal of 1785—when it was granted the duty on sedan chairs—it plaintively states "that for some months past sixteen of the beds have been occupied by double patients." It was then seriously contemplated turning the colourful chapel into a ward. Even up to 1890 we find that the staff nurses, nurses in-training, and wardsmaids were obliged to sleep in the same wards with the patients, and there were no diningroom facilities. Cleanliness and hygiene were then beginning to receive more attention, as the Hospital at that time had not even one bathroom. In 1904, due to excessive admissions, patients had to be accommodated on stretcher beds or admitted to the gynaecological wing. Then it was the practice for mothers to be discharged eight days after their confinement, which distressed Her

Gracious Majesty, Queen Alexandra, who intimated to the
Hospital her desire that the period be extended to fourteen
days which applied to the London Hospitals. I wonder would
the present hasty discharge from the London maternity
hospitals cause her to frown.

We are a people who pay the greatest tribute to our patriots
that have given the most sensational colour to our history
and have bowed to the most dramatic curtain from the stage
of life. Dr Mosse cannot be included in that flamboyant
category, but our people owe him an enormous debt of grat-
itude, and glorious remembrance for being the first person in
these Isles to focus the limelight on the "Massacre of the
Innocents." It is impossible to imagine the dizzy heights that
he might have reached in the social sphere of wealth if he had
concentrated his organising ability and genius in that direction,
instead of listening to the harrowing cries of the premature
dying infants of the Dublin slums. That frail, tiny light of
Hope that he ignited in a makeshift hospital in 1745 still
blazes brilliantly in its Rotunda home—an inspiration and
encouragement to those who have faithfully followed his
guidance and handed it more blazing to posterity.

Now, when I stare through the garden's railings, there
arises a pang of sorrow when I visualise that, as a child, I
played with my coloured green ball on its green slopes, and
romped under the yellow lanky laburnum blossoms, or the
pink and white flaking hawthorn branches, or the purple
clustered lilac. They are gone. So are the gravelled paths
where I rolled my wooden hoop, and which were bordered
by dainty flower-beds from which I picked the waxy-
stemmed bluebells for the Virgin's May altar. That little hill
is still there which I waddled up to lean against its queer
stone obelisk and look over the high spiked railings at the
bowler-hatted cabmen in their black frieze coats, from which
dangled their crude enamelled registration plates, anxiously
awaiting a customer, their eyes focussed on the Hospital
entrance for the discharge of a proud mother, escorted by
her attentive husband, closely followed by the beaming nurse
carrying the carefully wrapped new-born infant; or for the
sudden shout of a red-faced cattle dealer demanding a hurried
lift to catch the Galway train from the Broadstone Station.
Some of the blinkered horses were dozing away, their noses

streaming wet, others were chewing oats from the sacks
strewn on the cobbled street, jerking their heads to frighten
the chattering fluttering sparrows which hovered around
their meal. There still remains in the centre of the grounds a
few granite stumps from which once reared the giant-like
iron lamps which cast their yellowish glowing beams on the
dusky evening's lingering shadows. Now the mighty Rotunda
buildings have crept up on the hill, sweeping away the land-
marks of the fading past, like footprints on the sands of time.

At the top of the Gardens—where once floated the strains
of dreamy music and where rushed hither and thither in
genteel confusion the gold and rainbow coloured sedan chairs
with their silver embroidered tasselled curtains—there now
stands a nation's tribute to her glorious dead, guarded with
its golden gates entwined with silver harps, its shimmering
sunken pool reflecting the soaring Swan-Children of Lir.
Here in the circling seats one may laze, or read, or think, or
perhaps dream of that enchanting past. I wonder is a fleeting
thought ever given to that great humane unselfish Doctor who
bought that bit of marshy stagnant ground, and who now
lies in an unknown grave in a filthy discarded Donnybrook
graveyard.

5

Moore Street, 1916

When James Connolly dictated the following dispatch in the General Post Office to his trusted secretary Miss Winifred Carney—the only woman to have marched to his column from Liberty Hall with Webley in hand, beside his 16-year-old son, Roddy—did he realise what an important part this famous marketing street would play in the final days of the 1916 Insurrection? This was but one of the many dispatches she would type from the besieged headquarters. Beside her busy typewriter lay in readiness her loaded Webley. She was highly efficient in the use of arms having received her training with the Belfast Citizen Army:

Head Quarters—Army of the Republic—Dublin Command

26th April 1916

To the Officer in Charge, Henry Street (Frank Henderson).
    Erect barricade in Henry Street—both sides of Moore Street.
    Occupy first floor in houses taken in Henry Street and top floors also.
    See that the men are instructed to keep fire under control—not to fire on small bodies. In all cases wait for word from responsible officer before commencing to shoot. A few men should be placed in the end house on each side of Moore Street and Henry Street end.
    After this is done, find out what available food, water and utensils are at your disposal and report accordingly.
    Be sure to break all glass in the windows of the rooms you occupy for fighting purposes.

Commandant General
JAMES CONNOLLY (Dublin Division)

It was almost six o'clock on Friday, 28 April, in the General Post Office. Clarke, MacDermott, Plunkett and The O'Rahilly had gathered around the bed of the wounded Connolly to prepare a plan of evacuation from the burning building. In confused pity they gazed on their Commandant General as he winced in agonising pain. The previous morning he had been wounded in the arm while supervising the erection of a barricade outside of the GPO in Princes Street. That evening, when returning alone from the supervising of another barricade in Abbey Street, he had been felled by shrapnel, which shattered his ankle. Fearing to attract attention from the enemy, he inched his way back on one knee through Williams Lane, collapsing in the gutter, where he was assisted back to the GPO, and there he was attended to by the fifth-year medical student, Jim Ryan, and a British Army prisoner, Captain Michael Mahony. Splinting and first-aiding his ankle, they both agreed that it needed hospital attention. Scorning their advice, he ordered that his bed be positioned close to the main entrance under the portico, from which the fiercest assault from the enemy was expected.

Incendiary bombs had now landed on the sagging roof of the blazing building which was on the verge of collapse. Burning fragments and smashing glass were crashing through the curling flames onto the cinder-smouldering floor. The shaft descending to the crammed ammunition cellar would ignite at any moment. The wild suggestion of escape through the filthy choked sewers was impossible. Headquarters had lost contact with the main outlying positions. The enemy now had a clear field for military attack—one of their armoured cars had even advanced from Mary Street and returned after reaching Arnotts. They were trapped. It was agreed that their only chance of escape was through the Moore Street area, in the vague hope of taking up quarters at Williams and Woods factory in Parnell Street and perhaps, eventual escape—to where? Apparently they were unaware that Parnell Street was already under enemy control since Thursday.

First there had to be evacuated the 16 wounded, they hoped, to Jervis Street Hospital. Then 12 of the remaining women, who had stubbornly refused to budge, must be safely removed. The Volunteers commenced to break through the Henry Street houses to reach what they considered the comparative safety of the ultra-modern Coliseum theatre, which had been built the year previous, claiming that its 3,000

audience could be cleared out in three minutes. Five of the
tunnellers were of the Ring family. Quartermaster Desmond
Fitzgerald, Captain Mahony, and Fr Flanagan (who later was
to be canon at Fairview Church) were in charge of the evacuees. The priest had returned to the GPO on the previous
day at the request of Pearse. With a friend they were obliged
to detour through Thomas's Lane, Marlboro' Street, Parnell
Street, and while midway up Moore Street his companion
was shot beside him on the roadway, where the priest admin-
istered the last rites. Two courageous lads bore the dying
man to Jervis Street Hospital in a handcart.

Breaking through the buildings with the wounded was a
slow job, sometimes necessitating creeping on hands and
knees. A roof had to be scaled and then a ladder mounted to
get through the narrow bar window to the brief temporary
comfort of the theatre's carpeted floor. For days this white
marble-faced building facing Moore Street had been occupied
by weary volunteers, constantly under fire from the Parnell
Street barricade. One of them, utterly fatigued, was found—
with gun in hand—snoring on the window-sill.

Fitzgerald knew that soon the building would be afire—
like the adjacent Waxworks. So, after a short rest, a rear
breakthrough was made into Princes Street: behind the back
of Arnotts—and through Williams Lane, out into Abbey
Street. From behind a Liffey Street barricade, they were confronted by military pointing rifles and a yelling officer who
commanded their white flag bearer—with one other, to
advance. When Captain Mahony exposed his khaki uniform
it was the passport for negotiations—resulting in them
receiving safe conduct, to Jervis Street Hospital. Much credit
must be given to Mahony, who was the only doctor in the
GPO, and as a prisoner of war, was fully entitled to refuse
aid to their wounded. But then he was a Cork man.

The grim task of leading the first party in frontal attack on
the Moore-Parnell Street barricade, so as to divert the British
attention while the remainder tried to escape from the blazing
GPO, was undertaken by The O'Rahilly. He was a founder
member of the Irish Volunteers, a man of wealth, education
and culture, who resided with his family at elegant Herbert
Park. The previous weekend he had been Eoin MacNeill's
chief courier for cancelling the Rising. On the Monday,

when he saw the men that he had trained preparing for battle, he had no qualms that he must be with them. On arriving at the GPO, he was treated with the utmost scorn and suspicion—classified as a coward. It was five o'clock when he and his followers emerged from the side entrance in Henry Street.

They crossed the Moore Street barricade and divided on to each side of the street. Immediately they were the target for gunfire from the 6th Sherwood Foresters at the Moore-Parnell Street barricade scattering them for shelter in the narrow doorways. From the righthand side of the street Lieut. Strainger saw The O'Rahilly fall at the opposite corner of Sampsons Lane—apparently wounded. When the gunning had subsided, the O'Rahilly rose and gave the signal to the men on both sides of the street to advance. When about three-quarter way down he blew his whistle and gave another advance sign; rushing out into the middle of the roadway—sword in one hand and gun in the other—he collapsed in another terrific blast of gunfire from the barricade about 100 yards away. Behind him fell Pat Shortis of Kerry, Frank Macken of Rathfarnham, Henry Coyle of Dublin and Charles Corrigan.

Bullet-ridden, he dragged himself almost to the corner of Sackville Lane entrance where Volunteer Tom Crimmons, who although badly wounded made a gallant, but vain effort to assist him into the shelter of the lane. Eventually he managed to crawl to the steps of the doorway of Kelly's fish shop at the corner of the lane. Groping through his blood-clotted uniform he found a crumpled note from one of his sons, on the back of which he scrawled his dying words to his American wife. Parched—his blood oozing onto the cobblestones—he moanfully pleaded for a drink of water: the craved drink that never came.

At the opposite side of the street, at the corner of Riddles Row, Captain Seán MacEntee with 12 volunteers (four of them wounded) realised that further assault on the barricade would be suicidal, but, still hoping to reach the adjacent Williams and Woods, retreated through the laneways towards Coles Lane at the back of the slaughter houses. Now they were lost. Somewhere, they broke into a hayshed and found water where they attended to the wounded and consumed

their meagre rations. Darkness had descended; they must
wait until dawn to find escape. Utterly fatigued, confused
and despondent; drowsiness and uncalm sleep overcame the
bewildered scattered band. Of the 30 brave men who had
followed The O'Rahilly 21 were casualties.

It was after 7.30, in the Henry Street corridor of the GPO,
when the main body trampling through the deep smouldering debris assembled to prepare for retreat. Flying bullets to
them presented no terror compared to the crackling flames
behind and overhead. Beside the consumptive Joseph Plunkett was his aide-de-camp: Captain Michael Collins. The
previous Sunday he had dressed the frail invalid, and removed
him from Miss Quinn's Nursing home at Mountjoy Square,
where he was lingering from a severe glandular throat opera-
tion. By cab they went to the Metropole Hotel, where they
spent the night, the building swarming with British military
preparing for the following day's races. Little did the "hot-
headed" Collins realise that in a few years time £10,000
would be the price for his head—dead or alive.

At the intermittent signal of Pearse's sword the waiting
evacuees dashed through densely smoke-clouded Henry
Street, under heavy firing from Mary Street, into the lane
opposite—Henry Place. Pearse hesitated to follow the evac-
uating party but rushed back into the flaming building to
assure he was the last. Satisfied, he dashed out after them
but on glancing over his shoulder was horrified to see two
grimy-faced volunteers, in scorched uniforms, emerge from
the flame-licked doorway. Harry Boland and Diarmuid Lynch
had been overlooked in the treacherous ammunition basement.

When the party had advanced down Henry Place, and
turned left and about to cross the mouth of Moore Lane,
which ran parallel to Moore Street they found themselves the
target of machine gun fire from the military barricade in
Parnell Street facing the Rotunda Hospital. Snipers were also
firing from the tower of the Rotunda and Findlater's Church.
Temporary confusion seized the surprised volunteers com-
pelling them to scatter and dash to the safety of sheds and
stables. Plunkett, in one of his moments of renewed energy,
grasped and raised his sword and sternly commanded that a
barricade be immediately erected across the mouth of Moore
Lane. Ant-like they rushed to work. The basis of the barricade

being an old cab and cart over which they dumped empty crates from the adjacent mineral water factory. Volunteer Dickie Gogan here recalls Connolly snatching from him his rifle and ordering him to assist a wounded volunteer into one of the sheds. Dickie at fourteen had joined the volunteers and with his three brothers had fought the advancing military at Cabra bridge. They had a confectionery shop at the corner of Parnell-Dominick Street (now Johnston Mooney & O'Brien), where I had often bought my "hapny-worth" of sweets; in fact for a farthing you could buy the leavings of "crumbs". In the "Tan" days it would be one of Collins's frequent "dens", with that of Kirwan's pub across the road, and continually raided. Dashing behind the makeshift barricade, the volunteers, with the three women, eventually reached the far side of Henry Place—a few yards from Moore Street corner. They piled into a small yard, with their 14 wounded, fronting McKane's cottage. One of the volunteers in a clumsy effort to burst the lock of the cottage door, shot Mr McKane, who was trying to open it, carrying a baby in his arm. The bullet passed through his shoulder—killing his 15-year-old daughter, Brigit. Pandemonium seized the McKane household of 14 screaming children. The hysterical mother shouted: "My husband is dying: I must get a priest." Throwing a shawl over her shoulders and grabbing a pillowslip she burst her way through the perplexed volunteers trying to bar her way and rushed down Moore Lane waving her white "flag" towards the military barricade at Parnell Street, ignoring the shouting and cursing of the astounded soldiers. Shortly she returned to the amazed house-hold, accompanied by a young Dominican priest who went when he beheld the bleeding spectacle that confronted him. Sheets had already been snatched from the beds for the wounded, and willingly the McKanes hastily boiled the last of the sack of potatoes for the hungry volunteers. Mr McKane was hurriedly brought to hospital, where he spent 13 weeks. His daughter Rosie, who was the baby in his arms, told me recently that they never received a penny compensation.

The arduous task of attending the wounded was the lot of Nurse O'Farrell and her school friend, Julia Grenan. Both of them had been trained in the use of arms by Madame Markievicz at her cottage in the Dublin mountains. On the

Easter morning the nurse had taken dispatches to Liam Mellows in Galway, and Julia had brought dispatches to Patrick Hughes at Dundalk and Carrick-on-Shannon, during the week she and the 14-year-old Mary McLoughlin carried out several dispatches throughout the City. These two women had been friends of mine since I was 18—we were in the same class in the Gaelic League. I frequently visited her when living alone at No. 27 Lower Mount Street (now demolished). One had to be careful asking her about her 1916 activities, about which she was reluctant to speak. She smilingly commented about both of them being the only two women to arrive at the GPO armed with umbrellas! She could not remember getting a bit to eat or a wink of sleep in the GPO. She proudly boasted that in her little fight she had helped to pull out a brick from the wall of British Imperialism. Before she died she gave me two of her books on 1916 signed "to my old friend Séamus—GPO and Moore Street 1916. Julia Grenan". Julia and Lizzie lie side-by-side at the edge of the Glasnevin Republican Plot. Both had refused to humble themselves to seek permission from "a Free State government" to be buried with their 1916 comrades. Éamonn Mac Thomáis gave the oration over each of their graves.

The volunteers now made an entrance into Coogan's shop at the corner of Moore Street, startling Mrs Coogan who was skinning a cooked ham. Willingly, we are told, she handed it over to the hungry uninvited guests, and with her husband hastily descended to the safety of the chilly basement. In the kitchen the leaders held a hurried Council of War. There it was agreed that the 18-year-old Fianna boy, Seán Mac-Loughlin be promoted to High Command. Under Seán Heuston at the Mendicity Institute he had displayed outstanding bravery, and at the GPO the leaders had recognised his ability for such promotion, a glowing tribute to Madame Markievicz's trained scouts. Miss Grenan recalls him kneeling and talking to the wounded Connolly and when he stood up saying: "James Connolly has given me his Command". He had been proposed by MacDermott and seconded by Connolly himself. I have been unable to ascertain the whereabouts of this lad after 1916.

Lieut. Oscar Traynor, who with his little band of soldiers had so heroically defended the Metro-Mansfield-O'Connell

Street block and had almost been overlooked in its evacuation, was now assigned the laborious task of directing
the tunnelling through of the Moore Street walls towards
Parnell Street. This work proceeded through the night's
darkness relieved only by the flaming light of the burning
buildings unaware when they would be confronted by the
enemy. McLoughlin posted sentinels around the territory,
and those with no special assignment were ordered to rest.
Sleep was doubtful. MacDermott and Jim Ryan briefly dossed
down on a mattress in the corner of Coogan's kitchen. Pearse
continually shadowed by his brother Willie—both lay on top
of a table, covered by their coats. Under them snored a
weary volunteer grasping his rifle.

At three o'clock they were all suddenly awakened. The
dreadful expected had happened: the GPO ammunition cellar
had exploded; rendering a spluttering volcano enveloped in
dense smoky clouds, which quaked the foundations of the
surrounding streets. Guarding a mock barricade, which had
been intended to extend from Henry Place across to Sampson's Lane, were Volunteer Frank Kelly and Captain George
Plunkett. Barely hearing feeble moans from the corner of
Sampson's Lane, and fearing that it was a fellow volunteer,
Plunkett dashed across Moore Street, amidst a volley of firing, to find that it was a wounded British soldier. Undoubtedly, with some hesitation, he hoisted him over his shoulder
and, rushing back, unceremoniously planked him in the safety
of Henry Place, and retraced the same journey to retrieve
the British rifle. Three of the Plunkett brothers would later
be sentenced to death.

We will now take a brief survey of Moore Street on this
historic Friday morning before the evacuation of the GPO.
Our house—No. 31 (since demolished)—was but one from
the corner of Parnell Street corner. On the previous day the
British Military had commandeered the two houses at Parnell
Street corner and erected a barricade (not without casualties) which extended to within a few feet of our shop. Every
shot from that barricade rattled our old unsteady windows,
and the thunderous flashing shells from the 18-pounder
shook the three-storied house as they whizzed past. Sniper
bullets had already riddled our top back room window. The
military had taken possession of our back yard. The arrogant

officer had haughtily demanded us to prepare for evacuation as it was their intention to level whatever houses were necessary to "root out the Sinn Féiners". It was a demand to us three little boys, aunt and uncle.

Over the adjoining butcher's shop resided the McGrane family, who were worried about their young brother, Joe, who was the junior sacristan in the Pro-Cathedral. The church was being licked by the flames from Cathedral Street, Earl Street and O'Connell Street, and the priests were preparing to have the sacred vessels removed to safety. Little the McGranes realised that their little Joe would give 50 years continuous service to the church, and would have the honour of being buried in its vaults under the high altar with the deceased priests and bishops. Their little niece, Rosie McEvoy, was sobbing about her brother, Tom, who on the previous Monday had left his Sampson's Lane home, uniformed, for what he assumed was a usual route march. Nothing had been heard of him since. They were unaware that he had been assigned to the GPO and with Mrs Sheehy Skeffington was carrying food etc, to other areas. Rosie, now 77, and writing me recently from America, where one of her sons is director of a bank, recalls that

> we had house-maid knees from continually saying the Rosary, and while on our knees the window was blown in, which made us scurry down to our tiny backyard. Later the military moved us over to O'Connor's two-roomed house at No. 30. Later we were transferred to No. 40 or 41 Parnell Street.

Earlier in the week, she recalled seeing one of the neighbours—a few doors up the street on the far side—holding up looters with a toy gun, and taking the stuff off them, and keeping it for his own use.

The Home & Colonial Stores was at No. 33. Earlier in the week it had been assailed by looters, "dickied out" in grotesque robbed regalia from O'Connell-Henry Street drapery stores. Previously they had broken into Tommy Keeley's stores around the lane; who hired out handcarts at a shilling a day, and used them to transport their hastily robbed "souvenirs". Now they squeezed groceries into already overflowing carts, while tattered barefooted kids—gorged in sweets—pelted one another with packets of tea and sugar, footballing tins of preserves into the roadway, to the delight of the grinning shawled "auld ones". A boisterous carnival of destruction!

Facing our shop was No. 30½—the two-roomed poultry shop of the O'Flanagans—which appeared to have been shoved in between the two adjacent houses. Four of the sons were out fighting that week in the Four Courts area. One of them, Mick, had returned from England a few weeks previous with old furniture in which was conceded arms and ammunition. His brother "Pad-Joe" was one of the gallant seven to have made their last stand in the famous "Reilly's Fort" at the corner of Church-King Street. "The Fort" had been under continual heavy fire and the ammunition was almost depleted. "Pad-Joe" made a successful sally to the stores—near the Fr Mathew Hall—but on his return was mowed down at the door-way of "The Fort" and his precious ammunition scattered on the roadway out of the reach of the waiting volunteers. He was 24 and left a wife and three children. In the early Abbey Theatre programme of *The Plough and the Stars* one of the volunteers was referred to as a "chicken butcher". When I recalled this to Sean O'Casey on a weekend visit to him at his Devon home, he said that "Pad-Joe was the person, but had forgotten the name". He recalled, often with his mother buying chicken necks and giblets in their little shop. Later their house would be used as a Republican post office, and be continually raided by the British military. From our top window, one night I saw Georgie O'Flanagan being dragged by yelling and cursing "Black and Tans" through the battered doorway of their shop—half dressed and bare-footed—flung into a droning Crossley tender. When the O'Flanagan brothers were being laid to rest in Glasnevin Cemetery the President of Ireland, with bowed head, stood reverently by the grave side—a worthy tribute to the volunteer chicken butchers. Also to fall in the battle of Church Street was Patrick Farrell, who lived around the corner in Parnell Street; a comrade of the O'Flanagan brothers. He was by trade a plasterer and had left the Volunteer movement after the split, but, like The O'Rahilly, joined his comrades when called to arms. He was 19 years old.

Four houses on each side of Moore Street—Henry Street end—were now afire. Lieut.-Col. Owens had ordered five

shells to be blasted "into a white house" from the roof of the
Sackville Street Club, as he had been informed that there
were about 100 Sinn Féiners there.

Mr Fee, fleeing from his flaming house at No. 59, with a
white flag in hand, was shot dead. On the roadway lay
stretched Mr and Mrs Dillon with their daughter from No.
8. Now the Doyle and McDonagh families, tenants at No.
16, feared that the chemist shop—Gore's, beside them
would catch fire and decided that they must try and seek
safety with their friends in the opposite lane. Mr Doyle
attached his wife's apron to an umbrella followed by seven
others (one carrying a child), they dashed out on to the roadway; immediately they were sprayed with bullets. Mr Doyle,
wounded, fell in front of his wife, who tried to drag him after
her, but she was also wounded before she reached the opposite pavement. The O'Carroll family from their door (No.
49. Tripe dealer and dresser, manufacturers of Neats Foot
Oil and Tallow) succeeded with the aid of a rope in pulling
them into their shop, already crammed with over 20 refugees.
It was apparent that Mr Doyle was dying. A Mr Gorman
agreed to make an effort to contact the military in Parnell
Street, which he succeeded in doing by slipping through the
back slaughter-houses and alley-ways, where he was instructed
to bring the families directly down Moore Street and was
assured of a temporary cease fire. Mrs O'Carroll, with a
white sheet attached to a long-caned duster, along with her
husband and three children headed the party. Mr Doyle was
carried in a blanket, followed by his wobbling wife supporting
her wounded leg with an umbrella. Reaching the barricade the
men were shifted into the already wrecked Home & Colonial
Stores jammed with other male neighbours. Welcome, even
though crowded accommodation, over the Harold's Cross
Laundry in Parnell Street was provided for the terror-stricken
women. Mr Doyle was brought to the Rotunda Hospital—
another addition to the non-maternity patients!

Mrs Union, of No. 45, had already vacated her house and
sought the safety of her daughter's house at Mountjoy Street,
worried about her newly-ordained son at Ringsend Church.
Her little Joseph, whom she had so carefully watched as a
crawling infant, playing on the saw-dusted floor of her
butcher's shop, would one day be a canon, and now at 95 is

the oldest priest in the Dublin diocese. (*He died since the paper was read.*)

But who would quell Mrs Plunkett's anger when she'd return to her house at No. 16 and find her dainty back garden of budding spring flowers pulped into the ground? And, worse still, discover her front bedroom littered with butts of her blessed candles and her treasured linen sheets trampled on the floor and saturated in blood. Such a sacrilege! Never were they touched from the camphorated bottom-locked drawer only for the solemn ritual of laying out the dead. But she was far from annoyed—but proud to learn that the gallant Connolly had lain on her prided bed clothes and that the flittered ones had been utilised for the wounded volunteers.

At daybreak, the worn-out volunteers who had been wall-tunnelling throughout the night, reached No. 16, Plunkett's poultry shop. It was a tortuous task transferring the wounded through the narrow holes and crude entrances at different levels—particularly Connolly on the stretcher with his agonising gangrenous foot. Brian O'Higgins and his squad were allocated the delicate task of transferring the minor wounded down to the backyard to the slight comfort of an open hayshed. The volunteers still continuing their burrowing and scaling the outer walls towards the lane eventually reached the rear of Kelly's shop at the corner of Sackville Lane (now O'Rahilly Parade), where outside lay The O'Rahilly. The Kelly family have been maligned for not giving The O'Rahilly his craved drink of water. His cries and moans—even if heard—could have been that of a drunkard or looter, and to open a door or shadow a window was to risk death. Already a woman at the opposite side of the street, near to Riddles Row, had been shot dead while stooping by her bedroom window. Volunteer Crimmons recalls that he was informed that The O'Rahilly was still alive on the Saturday morning; so it is even possible that some of the volunteers in Kelly's yard could have heard his dying moans.

MacDermott and MacLoughlin now sneaked out from Kelly's yard and cautiously, from the corner of the opposite pub, surveyed the Parnell Street barricade. Returning to Kelly's yard they arrived at a new plan. Here they picked 20 volunteers—complete with baynotted rifles. Their idea was that the two of them would lead another frontal charge on the barricade during which they hoped that the main body behind would rush to safety through the alleys and laneways on the opposite side of the street. Among the 20 selected was the young Sean Lemass, who had assisted in carrying the wounded Connolly through the blazing GPO corridor. Already his senior brother, Noel, had been wounded in the Imperial Hotel. Another Council of War was held at noon in No. 16 around Connolly's bed—over which, ironically, hung a picture of Robert Emmet in colourful uniform, waving his curved feathered hat. The leaders listened avidly to the newly-hatched daring plan. Pearse, who through the shattered window had seen three men carrying white flags shot down, decided that they must surrender. Connolly agreed that the imminent risk of sacrificing further lives must not be tolerated. The leaders argued, wrangled and pleaded to convince themselves that the fight could be continued. But bitter reality just could not be ignored. Alluring heroics would have to be waived, no matter what the reluctance. They were defiantly faced with the ignominy of surrender. The frail grey-haired, 58-year-old Fenian, Tom Clarke, openly wept at the final decision. Conveying this pitiful message to the enemy was entrusted to the dauntless Nurse O'Farrell. With Captain O'Reilly's handkerchief tied to a piece of stick she passed through the doorway of No. 15 sprightly walking down the street of the dead. The military assisted her over the barricade and conveyed her to Tom Clarke's little shop in Parnell Street; there General Lowe demanded that within a half an hour she must return with Pearse to the Moore Street barricade, insisting that the only terms acceptable to him was unconditional surrender. It was 2.30 when Pearse, Willie by his side, shook each volunteer's hand in final farewell.

In his heavy military overcoat and Boer-shaped hat he marched down towards the barricade; the nurse almost trotting by his side. Here he was received by General Lowe, to whom he handed his sword, pistol and ammunition, also his tin canteen which contained two large onions. On the footpath, outside of Byrne's shop at the corner of Moore Street and Parnell Street, an old wooden bench, which was used for displaying pickled pigs' heads, was brought out from the shop; here Pearse stooped and signed the document of surrender which had been placed on it.

Elizabeth agreed to their joint request to deliver the documents of surrender to the various Dublin outposts. Without speaking and with that shy but charming smile with which he greeted the opposite sex, he warmly grasped her hand for the last time. Sorrowfully they glanced at each other as he was bustled into the waiting motor car. Seated beside him was General Lowe's handsome son, who would become a famous film star—John Loder, and be one of Hedy Lamarr's husbands. Hazily the nurse gazed after the car with armed soldiers hanging on to its sides on jolting sideboards, as it disappeared around the corner of O'Connell Street. She was the only woman, surrounded by enemy soldiers. We do not know what she was thinking about her leader, whom a professor had sneeringly referred to as "only a school master" and someone had said he was a poet "who was riding a winged horse".

At Moore Street headquarters the volunteers were stunned on learning the terms of the surrender. Most of them insisted on fighting to death. But Connolly was adamant: his boys must not be burned to death. Volunteer Seamus Devoy, nephew of the famous Fenian, now returned to No. 16 informing them that he had made the necessary arrangements to have the Parnell Street barricade opened to receive Connolly. Many years later I would have the pleasure of acting with Devoy with the Edwards MacLiammoir Co., but was unaware of his 1916 associations. Jim Ryan renewed the bandages and attended to Connolly's foot, Julia combed his tattered hair, and the devoted Winifred tidying his dust-covered Citizen Army uniform burst into tears for the first time—unable to control her grief: they dripped down on to his dark green jacket. He distressfully looked on the four wounded soldiers—one of them British—huddled on an old mattress in the corner, from the danger of the barricaded gaping window, as they hoisted his stretcher through the kneeling soldiers—balanced by their rifles in one hand. In the other hand dangled their rosary beads which they numbered in monotonous murmuring prayer.

In the narrow hallway of No. 15 they had much difficulty with Connolly's stretcher. Christy O'Leary, who was looking through the window of his house opposite in No. 47B, recalls that about 6.30 he saw Connolly being assisted through the doorway, supported by a stick and sweeping brush. Regally six volunteers bore his stretcher down the street; one of whom was Seamus Devoy. Captain Diarmuid Lynch (who would be condemned to death) headed the sombre procession as it echoingly clanked over the stone pavements. On 12 May the dying Connolly, propped-up and tied to a chair, faced the British firing squad. A few days later in the British House of Commons the Under-Secretary of State for War, would state: "Although Connolly was unable to walk, there was no reason why, in the interest of humanity, the execution should be delayed."

The wounded were now carried out in blankets through the narrow hallway and placed on the street pavement propped against the walls of Hanlon's fish shop to be collected an hour later. Captain Breen and Willie Pearse then searched the lane and alleyways for any scattered volunteers and marched them back with Sean MacEntee's little group. Sean McLoughlin writes that over 320 volunteers lined up in Moore Street to the amazement of the surrounding British soldiers. Filing up and forming ranks, with sloped arms, the first group marched off under Captain O'Reilly, picking up any stragglers on the way. Next Willie Pearse headed the main body victoriously waving his white flag as if rousingly leading his Scoil Éanna boys in colourful pageant. Still, how insecure he must have felt without his brother by his side. At the court-martial he would condemn himself to death by his defiant attitude that he had been totally immersed with his brother in the Rising plans. Anyway, he was Pádraig's brother and the government was determined that he should also die.

Close behind Willie walked the determined Tom Clarke, continuously haunted by the 16 years of English convict imprisonment, but still as courageous as ever. That night those haunting memories would be vividly recalled when he would be stripped naked for a hideous personal search by the military.

Towards the rear, limping on his stick, followed the polio-stricken Sean MacDermott in navy blue suit, probably the handsomest and most jovial of all. Perhaps he was wondering the whereabouts of his fiancée, who had been evacuated from the GPO; Mary Ryan, the sister of his comrade Jim. Later she would wed Dick Mulcahy—now gallantly facing the British forces somewhere in the Fingal area.

Falling back in the rear, his neck heavily swathed in bandages—unbalanced by his dangling sword—and supported by Julia and Winifred—straggled the languishing Joseph Plunkett, the unique strategist with the spiritual poetic mind, who should have been wed the previous weekend. On the eve of his execution in a gloomy prison cell by the flickering light of a wobbling candle in a jam jar, he and Grace would be blessed in marriage.

Up Moore Street, around Henry Place and into Henry Street marched the clattering exhausted army. Amazed, their blinking eyes joyfully beheld the grim-skulled GPO still crowned by the limped tattered tricoloured flag, faintly flapping in the dusky evening's haunting glow.

Oh! Weary Warriors, your sleepless nights are passed. Peaceful be your slumber with your butchered comrades; cradled in your golden dreams of unfettered freedom. Farewell! Happy dead, unshadowed by the advancing billowing clouds of sour, bitter, bloody strife. In defeat you have won a glorious spiritual victory. You have stirred the nation's drowsy heart and "redeemed Dublin from many shames, and have made her name splendid among the names of cities". Farewell!

6

The Abbey Theatre 1916 Plaque

It is amazing how the obvious can be ignored. This particularly applies to the Abbey theatre 1916 plaque which is conspicuously placed on the opposite wall facing the patrons as they bustle through the glass door entrance. So many have never noticed it, and if they did, the names inscribed on it convey very little. Hence the object of this paper.

The plaque was unveiled by the then Taoiseach, Seán Lemass, during the opening week of the new theatre, 23 July 1966. Only one of the survivors attended in an invalid chair—Helena Molony. The other, Arthur Shields, was spending his closing years in a sundrenched foreign land, with but dimming memories of his youthful Abbey acting years.

The plaque bears the following seven names—Ellen Bushell, Sean Connolly, Máire Nic Shiúbhlaigh, Helena Molony, Arthur Shields, Peadar Kearney, Barney Murphy.

MÁIRE NIC SHIÚBHLAIGH

In the Abbey vestibule, surrounded by a large gilt frame, hangs a painting by Jack Yeats (Sen.). It is of an extremely handsome, oval-faced lady, with clasped hands, and a black veiled dress reclining in an armchair. This is Máire Nic Shiúbhlaigh (Maire Walker) who was the first leading lady of our National Theatre. It was at her home in 56 High Street Dublin—where Wolfe Tone had been waked—that the first seeds of that theatre were sown. Her family were strong Parnellites and continually harassed for their national views.

In 1899, Yeats, Lady Gregory and Edward Martyn founded the Irish Literary Theatre. After producing seven plays—in its existence of two years—it collapsed, chiefly due to concentrating solely on English players who were unable to impress an Irish audience with their harsh foreign accent. After its demise the Walkers, the Fay brothers, AE (Russell) and Padraig Colum, who had been associated with Maud Gonne's Inghinidhe na hÉireann (The Daughters of Ireland) dramatic movement, gathered at the Walkers' home and discussed the founding of a National Theatre to be composed solely of Irish players. Neither Yeats nor any of the founders of the defunct Irish Literary Theatre were in any way involved in these discussions.

Their first production took place at Dublin's 300-seater cramped Saint Teresa's Hall on the night of 2 April 1902, under the title of W.G. Fay's National Dramatic Society, when they performed AE's *Deirdre*, in which he took part, and also Yeats's new play, *Cathleen Ni Houlihan*, which he allowed them to produce on condition that Maud Gonne, for whom he had written the play, would take the lead. She was recognised as the most beautiful woman in Ireland. Her portrayal of Mother Ireland that night enchanted the packed audience, whose ears were stunned by her sensitive lilting of Yeats's subtle verse. Her dignified figure personified all that was graciously noble to the Irish national mind. Máire and the two Fay brothers appeared in both plays; her name was printed in Irish—the first time that an actress's title had appeared in that language on a theatrical programme. Yeats and Lady Gregory were in the first night's audience. They were enthralled with the performance.

Shortly afterwards the National Theatre Society was founded. Yeats was elected its first president, Maud Gonne and Douglas Hyde, vice-presidents, and Willie Fay, general manager. The Fay brothers were to prove its life blood, with their experience of touring around the country with inferior English melodrama. It was their ambition to portray to their audience the characters of the Irish people. They had amassed an intimate knowledge of stage draft, and evolved a unique style of voice control which obviated unnecessary stage movement, and concentrating on the power and beauty of speech. It was to be the demise of the vulgar-mouthed stage Irishman.

Their early performances were confined to ill-equipped dingy halls, totally unsuitable for their polished talent, and discouraging to their increasing audience. Their movement would have petered out but for the encouragement of a wealthy English lady, Annie Elizabeth Frederica Horniman. She was astounded by their diverse talent, which had eclipsed anything that she had connection with in England. She contributed over-generously to their future productions, eventually procuring for them a site at the corner of Abbey-Marlboro' Street. Through her sole financial assistance there arose on this corner, on 27 December 1904, our first Abbey Theatre. Unfortunately, she quarrelled about the National view of the directors, particularly maligning the Fay brothers. It was a bitter breach—never to be healed. She solemnly gazes at the Abbey patrons from her painted portrait near that of Máire's.

On the opening night of the new theatre Máire and her brother appeared in three of the plays, two of her sisters were assisting in the front of the house, and her mother supervising the costumes which she had made from AE's designs. Yeats was captivated with the beauty of Máire's voice. Here he had found an actress who could interpret the magic of his delicate verse, and do justice to his Cathleen Ni Houlihan—even though it could not be compared with that of his beloved Maud Gonne. Sara Allgood was not in the early performances of the new theatre. Máire's first big role was that of Nora Burke in Synge's first play, *The Shadow of the Glen*. Her realistic interpretation of the peasant Irish woman shocked the audience. They considered it a slur on women's chastity. At that time, an actress playing an unpleasant character was classified as that type. Máire scoffed it off, accepting it as a trifling comedy. The shy author was completely perplexed that his first work should have caused such a commotion. Little did he realise the furore that another of his plays was to engender.

Later, the company was formed into a directorate and the players employed on a fixed salary—which was completely against its foundation rules. Maud Gonne and AE seceded from the newly-formed theatre, as also did Máire, her brother, and two sisters with many others, and formed a new company in which they joined with Count and Countess Markievicz and also James Stephens. In 1910 Lady Gregory persuaded Máire to rejoin the Abbey as they were about to tour America. It was a step that she later regretted; that unselfish co-operative spirit was gone, swamped with its commercial outlook. This was the first time that Máire had accepted payment for her dramatic talent, which was £2 per week, with the additional responsibility of the wardrobe. The American tour was an outstanding success, the golden lilting voices of Máire and Sara Allgood held their new audience spellbound. But the greatest unexpected sensation awaited them in Philadelphia; *The Playboy of the Western World* caused an uproar. The play was decried as immoral and obscene and the cast was arrested.

In 1912 Máire again left the Abbey and joined the newly formed "Irish Theatre" which was being directed by Thomas McDonagh, Joseph Mary Plunkett and Edward Martyn. This was situated in an 18th-century Harwicke Street building, which had originally been a Jesuit chapel. It had been given to them by Plunkett's mother, the Countess. It became a centre of drama activity, concentrating on continental plays, as well as Irish. Máire assisted MacDonagh with his productions at Pearse's Saint Énda's; an outstanding success was that of Pearse's Passion Play which they directed at the Abbey. Later Máire acted with "the Leinster Stage Society", founded by Willie Pearse and his sister. They performed at the Cork Opera House for a week. The foundation of the Volunteers now meant more serious work for Máire as officer in the Cumann na mBan.

On Easter Monday morning 1916, Máire and five other girls entered Jacobs' Biscuit factory, already under the command of her literary comrade, Thomas MacDonagh. The Volunteers had already smashed out the window panes and were erecting barricades—composed of sacks of flour and sugar instead of cement. Máire and her girls were designated the task of preparing more wholesome food than Jacobs biscuits and slab cake for the 140 men in the building and the surrounding outposts. It was a large garrison, containing a quantity of foodstuff, which it had been hoped could be distributed to the more scanty outposts. But of this there was little hope, as the factory had been surrounded by the military from early in the week. However, it was an important link in the republican chain owing to its great height enabling them to focus attention on the Ship Street military barracks at the rear of Dublin Castle.

After 1916, Máire travelled extensively over Ireland and England at concert venues on behalf of the Prisoners Dependants' Fund with Pearse's mother. Prior to the establishment

of Radio Éireann Repertory Company, she adapted, produced and played in Pearse's *The Singer*, which he had written
for her and her sister. It was the first play ever broadcast in
Ireland. Her last appearance in a play was in the late '40s at
the Ozanam Hall, Mountjoy Square, when she bid her final
farewell in *Cathleen Ni Houlihan*—still refusing to accept any
money for her professional talent. Her later years of married
life were spent in Co. Louth, still active helping amateur
dramatics. In November 1958 at the Drogheda Cottage Hospital she made her final exit behind death's misty curtain.

PEADAR KEARNEY

On the wall of No. 11 Lr. Drumcondra Road a plaque states
that there on the 12 December 1880 was born Peadar Kearney the composer of "The Soldier's Song". At 14 years of
age the wayward Peadar lost his father and the responsibility
of supporting his mother and the five younger members of
the family fell on his youthful shoulders. It meant years of
menial struggles in dead-end jobs until he eventually qualified
for the poorly paid work of tradesman painter. His boyish
mind had been influenced by the patriotic literary work of
Willie Rooney, which set the seeds of an unbounded love for
romantic Ireland which would later be reflected in his own
popular poems and numerous ballads—enlivened by his
deep knowledge of music. He could play the bagpipes and
the violin, and during his later imprisonment had made a
complete mellow fiddle.

He was devoted to the Gaelic language, and, in 1910,
eagerly volunteered to work with Peadar Macken on the des-
olate Tory Island, painting its 100 feet lighthouse in the
hopes that he would become more proficient in it. Dangling in
their swaying jack-cradles—propelled by the gushing Atlantic
winds—they conversed in Gaelic, while above screeched the
whirling gulls and below crashed the roaring waves over the
rugged rocks. To him it was all more thrilling than painting
the lofty-arched ceilings of some city church.

In 1904 he was helping to build the new theatre of the
Irish renaissance on the ruins of the old Mechanics, and the
adjacent grim morgue. For 12 years he would be actively
associated with its cradle of infant struggle. In 1911 he was

with the budding company on its first English tour; again
with them in Liverpool on their 1916 tour, when he was
informed of the approaching Rising. Had he not assisted in
the landing of the guns at Howth? Now he must return to
use them. With but a few shillings in his pocket, for a half
crown of it he secured a collier passage to Dublin. The vessel
encountered such turbulent sea and hurricane that he and
the other eleven passengers had to be battened down.

On Easter Monday morning Peadar set out from his
Summerhill home in his Norfolk green sports coat—so
similar to the Volunteer uniform. A service rifle dangling
from his shoulder over his belt of 200 rounds of ammunition, and on his back a haversack with three days' rations. At
Saint Stephen's Green his Battalion "B" Company was allocated to the Fumbally Lane malt distillery where they arrested
ten policemen. Later his Company was transferred to Jacobs'
biscuit factory, where their uniformed prisoners were allocated the menial duty of peeling potatoes. On two occasions,
with his squad, they had to transport food to the Stephen's
Green garrison and return with a load of rifles and bayonets.

In 1920, he was interned in Ballykinlar Camp, where he
scribbled his poems and ballads, including his famous march
"Rise". For the first time, his "Soldier's Song" was published in 1916 with the music of Pat Heeney. In 1926, Dáil
Éireann declared it our National Anthem. But it was not
until 1931 that he received the sum of £1,000 in lieu of all
rights, thus making it state property. Michael Collins paid
this tribute to Peadar: "Nothing that Ireland could give,
would be enough for the man who wrote 'The Soldier's
Song'".

SEAN CONNOLLY

The Abbey Theatre had arranged a revival of Yeats's *Cathleen
Ni Houlihan* for the Tuesday of Easter week. The leading
male role was to have been taken by Sean Connolly. However, on the day previous he was captaining his Citizen
Army Company to take over the City Hall, with his little
army of 16 men and 9 women, which included three of
his brothers and one of his sisters. As he marched out he
remarked to one of his comrades that he'd be dead within a

few hours. His fatal prophecy was to be fulfilled; he was the first Volunteer killed that day.

Connolly had been employed in the City Hall in the Motor Tax Office, and so was familiar with the building. The Angelus bell was ringing as they marched up Cork Hill. Six of his men were ordered to attack the Castle gate entrance, where they overpowered three of the guards—preparing a stew. Little did Captain Connolly then realise that in a building only 25 yards away was the Chief Secretary of Ireland, Sir Matthew Nathan, and the Chief Military Intelligence Officer, Major Ivor Price, who were studying plans to round up the rebels. In fact, if his force had been larger—as originally planned—they could have taken the Castle, as it was completely undermanned.

Entering the City Hall, Connolly directed a squad on to the ground floor, proceeding himself with the remainder to the roof circling the huge dome. His 15-year-old brother, Matthew—he positioned near him—sheltered by a stone pediment. The boy fingered his tiny Winchester .22 target rifle as he watched for the approach of any military detachments. Later, Matthew, who had not slept for two nights, noticed that his brother's arm was bleeding; hurriedly he fumbled through his first-aid kit and dressed the bleeding wound. Sean then ordered the fatigued boy down to rest—never to see him again.

At 1.40 p.m. a British consignment of 140 arrived at the Ship Street barracks and immediately concentrated fire on the City Hall. Bullets perforated the slates as they splintered down the roof edges—now the few soldiers realised that they were trapped. Shortly after two o'clock Connolly focussed his rifle towards the sniper in the Castle clock tower; he was too late: with his rifle he clanged down the slippery slates, mortally wounded. His grim forecast was too true. Of the original ten men in that little garrison, three were killed and two wounded. Connolly's body—with 70 others—was interred in the garden of Dublin Castle—mostly coffinless. Later he was reburied in Glasnevin Cemetery. At 32 years of age he had made the supreme sacrifice, leaving a widow and three young children.

He was a talented actor after he made his first appearance at the Abbey in 1913 and appeared in at least a dozen new productions and many revivals. Lady Gregory expresses her gratefulness "for his beautiful and distinguished work, especially in the tragedy of *Kincora* and the comedy of *The Lord Mayor*. On the back of a letter—while travelling in the train— she wrote:

> O branch that withered without age!
> Would we could see you where you're missed
> Step airy on the Abbey stage
> Play there "The Revolutionist"—
> Or fill with laughter pit and stalls
> With Bartley Fallon's croak and cry—
> What led you to those castle walls?
> We mourn you, Sean Connolly.

ELLEN BUSHELL

The first play I saw at the Abbey was through the kindness of Miss Bushell, who gave me a "pass" for the front row in the parterre—almost perched amidst Dr Larchet's musical trio. On that October night in 1927 I was spellbound as I watched T. C. Murray's delicate drama, *The Piper in the Fields*, which has never been revived; also the subtle comedy of Lennox Robinson's *Whiteheaded Boy*. This visit was to be the end of my fanatic film-going; I had been snared into a wonderland of magical voices and mesmerised by the wafting of the sensitive fairy.

I always called her Miss Bushell, to all her friends she was known as Nellie. She was but a slip of a girl of 16 when, as usherette, she was at the opening of the Abbey, in 1904. Little did she then realise that she would spend, in many capacities, her remaining 43 years in its service. Daintily clad in black frock and skirt, fronted by white-laced apron, dark stockings and shoes, which Lady Gregory had asserted was the most graceful attire for the Abbey usherettes, she was a dignified figure as she guided patrons down the few parterre steps to their seats, and courteously presented them with the buff-grey coloured programme.

What a pity that no record has been kept of her memoirs to supplement those of Lady Gregory's. Her early childhood had been associated with the Fay brothers' theatre, and her deep-rooted love of the drama world could be expressed as intelligently as any astute critic. Her loyalty to the Abbey was of a genuine sincerity that has lapsed into the romantic age. During its early crisis, when an audience of 20 was deemed as "a fair house" and a single hand-clapping might disturb the actors, she volunteered to have her payment of 1s. 6d. a performance reduced. A great sacrifice for one already on a meagre wage. Her little house at 19 Newmarket was the meeting place of her early theatrical friends, where they chatted into the early morn. Later it was a marked house, when it had become a haven of rest for her Volunteer comrades: one had but to pull the string through the lid of the letterbox which was attached to the door latch to gain entrance at any time. Here, in her spare time, she practised the weaving of poplin from threads of her own spinning—a traditional craft brought to the area by the Huguenot refugees.

One of her various Abbey duties was custodian of its library. Here she concealed the revolvers of her comrades when they sneaked in to see one of their favourite plays. Proudly she recalled the night that her hero, Michael Collins, had risked going into the theatre to see a new play by one of his author friends. Suddenly the building was surrounded by "The Tans", cautiously she passed on to him the silent signal and in a few minutes had smuggled him out of the theatre under the noses of the enemy. She was then a member of his Intelligence Department. During the 1916 Rising she shouldered her rifle, as Peadar Kearney said, "like any man". She carried dispatches from the Marrowbone Lane garrison to Jacobs and the GPO. One of her most treasured possessions was the pencil which Pearse used to sign her return dispatch.

The Marrowbone Lane garrison held out until the Sunday afternoon of 30 April. The women were instructed—so as to avoid arrest—to escape through an adjacent tunnel. This they adamantly refused, defiantly retorting that they had come to fight with the men and only with them would they surrender. The little army of 22, chanting "The Soldier's Song", marched across Bride Street and there laid down their arms. As the women refused to sign a statement recanting their stand, they were interned for a week in Kilmainham Jail.

Nellie had the distinction of being awarded the 1916 and 1917-21 Service medals for her military activities in the

National Movement. During her last weary illness I used to visit her at the Adelaide Hospital, and was surprised that she had so few callers. Shortly before she died, she asked me to request one of her old Abbey friends to come and see her. But her "friend" only found the time to attend her funeral.

On an August morning in 1948, her tri-colour covered coffin was carried into Mount Jerome cemetery. Many of her old comrades, now in high places, were missing—those who had often jerked that string of her Newmarket letter box. Nellie's coffin was lowered to the rattling of blank bullets and the mournful dirge of the Last Post. She was but another of the now forgotten rank and file who had answered to the call of Cathleen Ni Houlihan.

ARTHUR SHIELDS

On the evening of the first day of May 1970, a coffin, draped with the tricolour, was carried through the portals of Saint Patrick's Cathedral. It was the final return of Arthur Shields, from far-off Santa Barbara, to his native city. He was one of eight children born to an Irish father and a German mother residing at North Great George's Street. At 14 he had been an odd-job boy at the *Evening Telegraph*, and later worked at Maunsells the publishers. In 1914, he, and Maureen Delany, joined the Abbey Theatre at £1 per week, where he would remain for 22 years, playing leading roles, including the first productions of Sean O'Casey's plays and joining them in their American tours. He was the first *Playboy* that I had seen, and still think he has not been eclisped. Probably his greatest role was that of Canon Skeritt, in *Shadow and Substance*, which he played a year before he left on temporary leave, to act in an American film production by John Ford of *The Plough and the Stars*.

While later filming in New York, he collapsed from TB. For health reasons his future had to be confined to a warmer dry climate. John Ford was intrigued with Arthur's unique style of acting, so different from that of his brother Barry Fitzgerald, which led to him appearing in numerous films— *Long Voyage Home, Drums Along the Mohawk* and *The Quiet Man*. Probably his outstanding film was that of Jean Renoir's Indian setting, *The River*. After the death of his first wife, he married the Abbey actress, Aideen O'Connor, who had appeared with him in *Shadow and Substance*.

In 1914 he had joined the Dublin Brigade of the Volunteers of which Oscar Traynor was the O/C. On Easter Tuesday of 1916 he was to have appeared in the Abbey's new play *The Spancel of Death*. This had to be cancelled, and has never been revived. On the previous day he marched into the General Post Office and during that week was continually on the alert between the buildings on both sides of O'Connell Street and constantly dashing across the street through the hail of bullets from the South Side of the Liffey, particularly from Trinity College and the Ballast Office.

With six others, two of whom were trained operators, he was designated by Joseph Plunkett to take possession of the Wireless School of Telegraphy in O'Connell Street close to Eden Quay, with the view of reassembling the disused wireless apparatus on top of the building. It was an impossible task, and they were obliged to return to the GPO, where Connolly instructed them to again recross the street, with the further task of erecting a barricade across the entrance of Lower Abbey-O'Connell Street to counteract any military activity from Amiens Street station. The work involved the dragging and erecting of huge reels of newsprint from the *Irish Times* warehouse. Upon these were topped dozens of brand new motor bikes, which were later priced as £5,000. In this laborious work they were constantly harassed by a violent anti-rebel mob. After his arrest Arthur Shields was interned in Frongoch Camp in Wales.

HELENA MOLONY

On an August evening in 1903, as the teenage Helena was strolling past the Custom House, she found herself on the outskirts of a public meeting being addressed by Miss Maud Gonne. Helena was stunned by this willowy figure with her mane of burnished bronze hair and the enchanting lilting voice, who epitomised those mystical figures she had visualised from the writings of Dr Douglas Hyde. Before the meeting had finished Helena had decided that she must join Miss Gonne's organisation—Inghinidhe na hÉireann. Later Maud Gonne would make her secretary. In 1908 she became editor of Maud Gonne's monthly magazine, *Bean na hÉireann*, which advocated feminism, separatism and militancy, a huge undertaking for a young girl unskilled in journalism. The following year Helena would accept a further engagement, the forming of Madame Markievicz's Fianna Éireann Boy Scouts.

In 1909 she was approached by the Abbey directors about joining their theatre, which she accepted. In spite of her political activities, she remained with the theatre for ten years, to be ranked among its foremost players. In one of the productions she appeared only in the first and last acts, and she availed of the break to sneak out—in her "make up"—to address strikers' meetings at Liberty Hall down at the corner of the narrow lane at the back of the Abbey. She appeared in at least 15 new plays and many revivals. Her last appearance was in 1919, when she acted in Desmond Fitzgerald's new play, *The Saint*.

In 1911 she was arrested as a protester against the royal visit of King George, having flung a brick through a Grafton Street window which was displaying a royal portrait. There was a wild scene in the court when she refused to pay the imposed fine of 40*s*. and was sentenced to a month's imprisonment. After serving some days in prison, her fine was paid by Anna Parnell, whose history of *The Ladies Land League* Helena was editing. On her release a huge public meeting awaited her, at which pandemonium broke out when the infuriated police again rearrested her for again attacking the character of the king. During the lock-out strike of 1913, she was second-in-command to Madame Markievicz in the running of the soup kitchens in Liberty Hall for the strikers and their families.

In 1915, when active preparations were in hand for the Insurrection, James Connolly appointed her secretary of the Women Workers' Union. Thus began her close association with the Labour movement; which was to continue to the end of her days. Helena held her commission in the Citizen Army and, as she marched out from Liberty Hall on Easter Monday (she had spent the previous night lying on old coats in the Hall), James Connolly pressed into her hand a revolver to be used in emergency. When the contingent arrived at the City Hall, which they were to occupy, it necessitated the women climbing over the iron gates.

In the caretakers' rooms Helena set up the women's quarters. As the day passed the building came under violent siege from the military. After two o'clock Helena, with two other women, dared to venture on to the roof with food for the defenders. Crouching around the dome towards Captain Connolly, when within a few feet of him, she saw him raise his rifle, immediately a shot ran out, the Captain jerked, slumped and collapsed. He was the victim of a sniper's bullet. Crawling to him, she cradled his head in her arm and breathed an Act of Contrition in the dying man's ear. With the assistance of Dr Kathleen Lynn, they both succeeded in dragging him down from the bullet-spattering roof.

As the night crept on, the ground floor was in pitch darkness, the din of the attack became deafening as the bullets spattered like rain, plaster thudded down from the ceiling and dust and mortar whizzed through the building. They gazed towards the rattling dome—any moment it would collapse. Death was hovering all around. Suddenly, there was a mighty explosion, the military had blown a huge entrance through the back wall of the City Hall; swearing and cursing, with fixed bayonets they swarmed into the building. The officer with a gun in hand called on them to surrender. To his amazement a woman stepped forward. It was Dr Kathleen Lynn, the only officer remaining. The military rounded up the handful of Volunteers who had so defiantly kept them at bay. The prisoners were taken to Kilmainham and detained there for six weeks—where each morning they listened to the volleys that martyred their leaders.

Of the 77 women arrested, Helena was one of the seven deported to imprisonment for life. However, at the Christmas amnesty, she was released. In 1921 she opposed the treaty, suffering further imprisonment from her former comrades. Later, the Irish Labour movement honoured her by the appointment as President of the Irish Congress of Trade Unions.

When I visited her, shortly before her death, she proudly displayed to me a delicately wooden hand-carved bellows made by Madame Markievicz. Helena had presented it to the National Museum complete with an engraved brass tab. As the museum found it impossible to put it on display, she demanded its return. Where is that bellows now? Perhaps lying in some heap of forgotten junk!

Emotionally, President de Valera—his wife by his side—
spoke at the grave of the 83-year-old Helena, on the last day
of January 1976:

> Helena was one of the greatest patriotic women of our
> time. With James Connolly and Madame Markievicz
> she worked for Irish Freedom—for the workers and the
> poor. She stood firmly for the rights of women and
> their political equality in our society. She was admired
> and beloved by those who knew her as a noble Irish-
> woman who had deeply at heart the welfare of the
> Nation. May she long be remembered amongst us.

BARNEY MURPHY

I have made most extensive enquiries about the above, who
was working as a stage-hand at the Abbey Theatre in 1916,
and shouldered his gun with his theatrical comrades. Regrettably, in spite of my minute searches, I have been unable to
ascertain where he was garrisoned during the Insurrection
period.

7

Dublin's Historic Hollywood

It is surprising that such a beautiful part of Co. Dublin as Hollywood, which is less than 20 miles from the city, a few miles from Swords, and only a mile off the bustling main Balbriggan/Belfast road, is almost unknown to the city dwellers. One gets the reply as to its whereabouts that it is in Co. Wicklow, or one is referred to the outskirts of Belfast, or to the west coast of the United States, a suburb of Los Angeles associated with motion pictures.

Here, hundreds of years before Saint Patrick lit his Paschal fire on Slane Hill, hefty warriors trudged up the steep hills of Hollywood—on the far distant curved shore there had not yet arisen the wattled cabins of the future Dublin. Later, its peaceful valley would echo to the chantings of white-robed monks. Its past should not be forgotten.

Overlooking this valley is the 600 ft. summit of Knock Breac (Speckled Hill), which is higher than the Hill of Howth. Its strenuous climb is certainly rewarding for the breathtaking panorama surrounding its summit. To the north, we can observe Slieve Gullion in Co. Armagh, the Mourne Mountains in Co. Down, Clogher Head in Louth, while dotted along the whitening sea curve are the towns of Rush, Portrane, Malahide and various villages. Towards the south, we see the widening expanse of Meath, Kildare and Dublin's fertile plains. In white-foamed Dublin Bay, the dainty islands of Ireland's Eye and Lambay are clearly visible—foregrounded by the twinkling lights of our great city.

Hollywood is best approached from the Naul/Kitchenstown Road, through the hilly fields of Farmer McDermot—who is ever willing to allow visitors to trespass and even, if necessary, take their cars up portions of the hilly land. We are now standing in the middle of one of the largest pre-Christmas hill forts, covering more than 21 acres. Its expanse is comparable to that of

Royal Tara. Even at this height, there is a sparkling spring of fresh water. Only in recent times, by means of aerial photography, has its magnitude been fully appreciated, as much of its surrounding ramparts have long since disappeared. It must be assumed that in those early days it was densely populated.

Around this fort are six tumuli; somewhat uniform in shape measuring in height about 12 feet, with a dimension of about 12 yards. Their definite outline is somewhat faint, as their outer ditches have become blurred through irregular ploughing and being trodden on by cattle. Three of them are within 50 yards of each other, and one of them is sited by a modern trigometrical pillar, which was erected in 1837. In a field overlooking the graveyard is a similar tumulus. From an exterior examination, they do not appear to have been ever interfered with. Comparing them with others of the same construction, they are estimated to be of early Iron Age—i.e. 600 BC to AD 500. If we are to accept the contentions of that brilliant antiquarian, Dr Petrie, this site is more ancient than immortalised Royal Tara, which, he asserts, only came into its glory between AD 200 and 300.

One wonders, in confused ignorance, what was happening here on those misty hills almost 2,000 years ago; and one can but hazily surmise the riddle of those weed-capped hillocks. Do they conceal some submerged tunnels similar to "The Four Knocks", a few miles away? Perhaps they cover clay urns sealing the ashes of cremated turbulent warriors slain in mighty battles in this area between the ancient Fianna and the native princes, so detailed in manuscript versions of Cath Gabhra of the Fenian Cycle. Maybe they were funeral pyres whose flames consumed the sacred remains of regal chiefs. Or were they just fiery beacons which linked the druidic instinct towards the twirling planets from whence they amassed their uncanny wisdom, which would, eventually, be subordinated and immersed in the ritual of approaching Christianity?

HOLLYWOOD GRAVEYARD

In the sloping Hollywood graveyard, there still stands the ruin of a pre-Norman church, built on the site on which Saint Canice founded his monastery in 557. In the levelling of its surrounds in 1833, there were unearthed (six feet below the surface) several clay urns containing ashes, which indicates that it was a burial place in pre-Christian days. The annals of Ulster state that the extraordinary Saint Canice was born in Dungiven, Co. Derry, in 525, the son of a wandering poet-harpist. Saint Adamnan, in his three books on the life of Saint Columcille (*Vita Sancti Columbae*) written shortly after his death, gives us intimate details of the monastic life of Iona and also refers to the miraculous powers of Saint Canice, including control over the winds. Columcille and Canice both had studied under Saint Finnian at the famous Clonard Monastery in Co. Meath and, later, they resumed their studies at Glasnevin under Saint Mobhi. One story, whether true or false, has him translating the Gospels and when queried by Saint Columcille as to how he had arrived at their interpretation, he replied "The Lord Jesus had come to me and read with me and taught me this sense of it." In 565, he had joined Columcille at Iona monastery and, later, travelled with him on his missionary crusade throughout the Hebrides. Saint Canice made numerous conversions in Scotland.

On the island of Iona, there are the remains of a ruined church and cemetery dedicated to him. On the shores of Lough Laggan, there is the ruin of a church, named Laggan Keith, and one of the beautiful isles of the Hebrides bears his name in its ruined church of Inch Kenneth. His feast day, 11 October, is still celebrated in the Scottish diocese of Saint Andrew and in Argyle. His name is grouped with those of our three national saints and the name Kenneth is the most popular in that area. Saint Canice, like Saint Columcille, was a poet and many poems remain, which were attributed to them. Besides the ruined church in Hollywood, the ruins of two remain in his own county of Derry. There is also the ruin of one in Finglas churchyard and the new church recently erected in that town is named after him. The little church down the road from Hollywood is also named after him. His most beloved church was the one he founded at Aghaboe, Co. Laois, in 577, in which he was laid to rest 12 years later. Like his Hollywood church, it was continually desecrated; firstly, in 913, and rebuilt in 1052; plundered again in 1116, and rebuilt in 1234, housing the sacred shrine containing his revered relics. Twelve years later, it was again plundered and the blessed relics destroyed by the Irish chieftain, Dermot FitzGerald. The last church to be built on its foundation was by one of the FitzGerald family for the Dominicans in 1382. The scanty ruin of its destruction in 1786 is now all that remains of the saintly Canice. However, but a few miles away, in the city of Kilkenny, towers the magnificent cathedral of his name, built on what it is believed was originally one of his church foundations.

HOLLYWOOD CHURCH

The ruin of Hollywood church, with its surrounding graveyard, in the beautiful valley is most impressive and of much historical interest. In a book I have seen, it is referred to as a miniature Glendalough, without lakes—more than a little exaggeration. Particularly of interest are the projecting stone steps ascending to the triple-arched turret in the west gable, up which the monks climbed to hammer out the different chimes on the tongueless bells. In the wall beside the curve-topped door are the remains of a damaged stone water font. How many centuries have elapsed since its blessed waters were rippled by a pilgrim's fingers? It is probable that, during this period of religious fervour, the area was referred to as "Holywood". Earlier it was probably referred to as the "Holly Wood", due to its abundance of this tree. Holly was considered a sacred plant by the druids and later its timber was preferred for the construction of harps, as it rendered a more delicate tone, and accepted a finer polish.

The chequered history of Hollywood Church is a confused one. Like many others in the area, adjacent to the city, it was plundered several times by the Danes and desecrated numerous times by the warring Celtic chieftains. With the advent of the Normans, it was grabbed by their greedy ecclesiastics from the original control of Dublin's Saint Mary's Abbey, and, by royal grant, it was submitted to the jurisdiction of the Cistercians of the Lantony Priory, in Gloucestershire, who readily appointed their own Norman vicars to the stolen churches of Finglas. The first mention of Hollywood is in one of the Lantony Latin books, dated 1185, in which it is referred to as the Church of the Holy Grove (Ecclesia de

Sancto Nemore). In 1211, the book again refers to it as Holywood (Ecclesia de Sancto Bosco).

The only reference I can find to the rebuilding of the church is in Dalton's *History*, where he refers to the work being carried out by Sir John Hollywood in 1215. Archbishop Bulkeley, in his detailed *Account of the Diocese of Dublin* (1630) refers to the church being ruinous "and not above 12 people frequent Divine Service in the Parish". He also reports that the Naul Church was a ruin, so where were the services held? Shortly afterwards, it must have been rebuilt as it is recorded that it was plundered by Cromwell's troops in 1649. There is in existence a silver paten inscribed "Hollywood 1754", so we have to assume that the Church was then being utilised. In the Damastown parochial house, there is an ancient chalice with the inscription "This chalice belongs to Hollywood exclusively." Unfortunately, it is undated.

In a document dated 1813, signed and sealed by the Marquis of Drogheda, we find that the Revd Thomas Baker AM was appointed incumbent of Naul, Grallagh and Hollywood. But, as there was no Glebe house attached to the church, he was content to accept an additional £40 per year as house rent and reside at his Malahow home (two miles away) with its 300 acres. He died in 1857.

A document dated 18 September 1867 tells of the Protestant Archbishop of Dublin "exhorting the parishioners of Naul & Grallagh whose churches are ruinous, owing to the few people and who are unable to build them, to resort for public worship to the adjoining parish of Hollywood". This is rather strange, as a new church had been built in Naul in 1812. Old people of the area never heard their grandparents speak of the Hollywood Church ever being in use. In 1883, the Hollywood Church, being a ruin, was united with Clonmethan. Clonmethan Church is now a roofless ruin.

The oldest headstone traceable in Holywood graveyard is that of "Peter Flynn, 3rd March 1716, aged 96". But the oldest record of a burial is of John Kempe and appears in his will, made on All Saints Day in the year of our Lord 1471. The original will is in Latin. It reads:

> In the name of God Amen, I, John Kempe though weak in body yet sound in mind do make my testament in

this matter. First I bequeath my soul to Almighty God, the Blessed Virgin and all the saints and my body to be buried in the Church of Saint Canice, Hollywood.

It is interesting to note the value of his farm animals specified in the will:

7 cart horses worth	18s.	[now	worth	£3,500]
8 cows	"	32s.	["	"	£5,600]
3 heifers	"	5s.	["	"	£1,350]
4 hogs	"	5s. 4d.	["	"	£ 240]
12 pigs	"	6s.	["	"	£ 300]
34 sheep	"	11s. 4d.	["	"	£2,380]

We now find an interesting document dated 1788 in connection with the payment of tithes to the Archbishop of Dublin, being the humble petition of Revd John Echlin, vicar of the parishes of Naul, Hollywood and Grallagh in the said diocese: "That Edward Crilly of Newtown in the Parish of Hollywood in the County and Diocese of Dublin, Gent. was in the months of Sept/Oct. in the years of Our Lord 1785/6/7 possessed of 148 acres of corn and hay to the total tithes of £40. 4s. 8d., all of which corn and hay the said Crilly drew home without giving notice to or making any compensation with Petitioner who, therefore, prays that a citation may be immediately granted against the said Crilly for subtraction of the said Tithes. Dated this 27th day of May 1788."

THE HOLLYWOOD FAMILY

Towards the end of the 11th century, a Norman family by the name of de Maresco held extensive land at Hollywood. They are mentioned in a document of King John, dated 1206. "That Geoffory de Maresco holding fee at Hollywood and wondering if he had received it as a swop from the Archbishop of Dublin." Later, we find the name changed to Sacro Bosco, and later on to that of the manor where they dwelt: Hollywood. No trace of the manor, or its fortress foundation, remains. It is obvious that this family took its name from the area where they lived, and not the reverse, as is sometimes suggested. In 1230, the family had already taken the name of de Hollywood, as signed by John of that family, who had become a famous mathematician and philosopher on the continent and had written two masterly books on the subject. It is recorded that "he was buried with great pomp and ceremony in the Cloisters of the Parish convent of Saint Matierine, and that a sphere is engraved on his tomb." In 1310, Roger de Sacro Bosco (Hollywood) was summoned to attend the Parliament of Kilkenny, and 24 years later, Henry, a Dominican friar, was directed to parley with the O'Connor princes of the Irish in Connaught. Twenty-one years later, Robert was knighted for his loyalty to the Crown and referred to as "the worthiest then in chivalry". It is probable that, at this time, they acquired the lands of Artane, where they built their castle in 1390, referred to as Hollywood Castle.

Undoubtedly, they were loyal subjects of the Crown and there are many instances of their raids on the O'Tooles and O'Byrnes in the Wicklow glens. But there was no doubt also as to their loyalty and adherence to the old faith. Their services to the King saved them from molestation during the reigns of Elizabeth and James, but, like all Catholic gentry, they were precluded by the Test Acts from lucrative benefits and under the Acts of Uniformity they could have been victims of impoverishment. So it behoved all Catholics to be unduly cautious.

The most important of the family to us was Christopher, who was born in 1559, a year after Elizabeth's accession. His father, Nicholas, was then referred to as "the Lord of the Manor of Hollywood and Artane". Christopher, at the age of 21, renounced his heirship to this vast property to become a Jesuit, commencing his studies at the University of Padua. In 1598, the Pope appointed him as superior of the Order in Ireland, which had then dwindled to five priests. It was a difficult task to reach Ireland, as he had to undertake the circuitous route through Switzerland and Brussels, disguised as a merchant, but it did necessitate his taking a British vessel to Dover, where he was arrested, as he refused to take the oath of supremacy, even though he was accepted as a foreign merchant. He was imprisoned in the Tower, where he was again approached to take an oath that he would endeavour to persuade the Irish that it was unlawful for them to resist the

Royal Power's progress in their country. Imprisoned for five years and broken in health, he was released on the death of Elizabeth in 1603 "under the seal of Perpetual Banishment". The following year, he landed in Ireland to tend his scattered flock. His task was difficult, as, during the first half of the reign of James I, there were continuous intermittent persecutions, making it almost impossible to set up organised missionary work. The clergy, disguised as laymen, operated from private dwellings in remote parts of the country—their so-called "residences" only applied to a large district in which a number of Jesuits worked under a superior, but of no fixed abode. In 1619, he founded the first Jesuit School of Missions in Kilkenny. After 20 years of intense labour and missionary toil he died, leaving 42 priests to carry on his work. Before his death, he had the honour of being informed that he had been denounced by the King personally for the results of his missionary activity. Many of his philosophical works are extant, including his *History of Ireland under the Tudors*.

When the struggle broke out between Charles I and Parliament, the Hollywoods rallied to the King. Eventually, the Hollywood name figures prominently in the Black List of the Puritans. Later, Nicholas Hollywood's lands, consisting of 180 acres around Artane Castle and 760 situated at Hollywood, Damastown, Naptown and Gerrardstown, were grabbed by the avaricious Cromwellians and he and his family were banished to west of the Shannon. After the Restoration, portion of the plundered lands was restored to the Hollywood family, with the clause "only to the direct male heirs". In 1748, the last male heir died, and the lands were parcelled out to the King's favourite, Lord Granard, at the rent of three pence per acre. Later, the lands came into the possession of an absentee landlord, Lord Maryborough, who let them out at £4 to £8 per acre. His title became extinct in 1863, when the castle was demolished and replaced by a modern house, which still bore the name of Hollywood Castle. Here for some years resided Sir William Butler. In 1870, the Christian Brothers acquired the property, on which they erected their famous Industrial School.

The old Artane graveyard is now securely railed off with its crumbling old ruined church, which once sheltered the elaborate carved stone tomb of the Hollywood family. Now there are only a few fragments of the headstone, bearing faint traces of its intricate floral design and the stately coat of arms; the inscription is faintly discernible:

> This tomb has been erected by Christopher Hollywood of Artane, esq., 1711, the 10 Feb. Anno Domini. Underneath the same, body of Elizabeth wife to the above Christopher Hollywood, daughter of John Talbot. Malahide, esq., who departed this life 25th June 1711. Here also lieth the body of the above-named Christopher Hollywood esq. husband of the said Elizabeth who departed this life 12th Aug 1718.

A faint reminder of a noble family. Other less ornate head-stones of that period surround the Hollywood memorial: humble Dublin tradesmen, proud of their ancient crafts, a coach builder, a shoemaker, a stone cutter, a coal factor and a greengrocer from Ormond Quay.

We are indebted to Messrs Quinnsworth for the elaborate granite stone in front of the entrance to their supermarket indicating that this was the original site of Hollywood Castle.

THE MURDER OF ARCHBISHOP ALLEN

The castle acquired terrible notoriety during the month of July 1534, due to the foul murder of Archbishop Allen, who had been appointed to the Dublin diocese by Cardinal Wolsey six years previously. Allen had incurred the intense dislike of the Geraldines family, who were staunch Catholics. This bitterness developed into intense hatred when the FitzGeralds realised that the Archbishop was in sympathy with the attempts of King Henry VIII to crush the Catholic Church established in Ireland. Garret Óg, Earl of Kildare and King's Deputy in Ireland, had been summoned to London, leaving his 21 year-old son, the dandy, Silken Thomas, as his Vice-Deputy. Later, a false rumour, initiated by the Archbishop, was circulated that the Earl had been murdered in the Tower. Enraged, the impetuous youthful son, with a small band of armed retainers, marched on the Council Chamber at Saint Mary's Abbey (adjacent to the present Capel Street) and, before the amazed gathering, flung down his father's sword, which was the emblem of his official authority, and in a defiant speech accused the King of his father's murder, branding him as his eternal foe.

This was the beginning of his hasty, ill-fated rebellion, composed of Irish chieftains and Anglo-Irish nobles. The crafty prelate now realised that his life was at stake, and he hastily embarked on the night of 27 July from the little haven of Dame Gate to seek refuge in England. Unfortunately, the wind failed to favour the vessel and it drifted inland on to Clontarf Strand, from whence he tramped to Hollywood Castle, where he was willingly accorded sanctuary. The following day, the soldiers of Silken Thomas attacked the castle and dragged the unfortunate prelate outside and in the grounds cold-bloodedly stabbed him to death. In August 1535 Silken Thomas surrendered and, though promised pardon, in February 1537, with his five uncles he was hanged at Tyburn. Last year, when visiting the Tower of London, I discerned, among the graffiti of prisoners in the Beauchamp Tower, the following: "Gerald FitzGerald, 9th Earl of Kildare". A poignant reminder of the handsome immature youth who 450 years ago defied the tyrannical power of a ruthless English sovereign before his puppet Parliament in Dublin City. The spot in the grounds of Hollywood Castle where the unfortunate Archbishop was hacked to death remained derelict for centuries, sprouting a wilderness of briars and weeds; shunned in horror by the locals after dark until the castle was demolished.

The old disused slate quarry beside the Hollywood Churchyard once gave high hopes for the creation of ample employment for all the unemployed men of the area, if we are to heed *The Irish Builder*'s report of April 1868. This mentions the then recent visit of several distinguished architects and engineers, who were convinced that the quarry contained good slating, and they expected to form a company with a view to its development, believing that the material would be a boon to the city. Eventually, they expected it to give employment to close on 200 workers. This rosy future never materialised. Today, it looms as a pit of dismal decay.

THE HOLLYWOOD MURDER

On the evening of 10 October 1864, the peacefulness of the Hollywood hills was shattered by the frightening echo of a most brutal murder. The Press reported that "it was a murder as horrible as has been recorded in this century". When Richard Murphy returned to his 13-acre farm cottage after the "tip of sunset", he was horrified to stumble over his sister Ellen's battered body on the stone floor of the kitchen in front of the "rush fire". He immediately summoned the neighbours. Where was his sister, Ann? In a field, up the lane facing their cottage, Ann's hacked body was found where she had been milking a cow. Soon the constabulary were on the scene from the Ballyboughal barracks. Nothing was missing from the home, where the family had lived on the best of terms with their neighbours. It was apparent that both sisters had been slain with a weapon similar to a pitch fork—three of which were found in the attic and one, which had been recently cleaned, in the barn, but none of them could be linked with the crimes. Much importance was attached to the neighbours' report of hearing excessive moaning and snarling of the Murphy's dog, on passing the cottage that evening. Later, the dog was "hanged", as "he was going mad", apparently the sole dumb witness of the slaughter.

Murphy, who could neither read nor write, denied that he had seen his father's will, which was later produced from a locked box. The farm had been left to Richard; fifteen pounds to each of the sisters (roughly £600 in today's value) and to the remainder of the family, "one shilling each and no more", which could have bought each of them about five pints of beer. Richard was arrested for the murders. Six weeks later, both bodies were exhumed for further examination in a nearby shed. The trail lasted a week; the judge taking four hours for his summing-up. In less than an hour, the jury returned a verdict "not guilty" which received great cheering and applause from the public gallery. Shortly afterwards, Murphy married, bringing his bride to the ill-fated cottage, where their two children died in their teens.

One dark night, after the murders, when the priest and "his man" were about to drive past the cottage, their horse suddenly halted, and stubbornly refused to budge. It was only when the priest dismounted and covered the animal's eyes and led him past the cottage that the horse moved and then furiously galloped down to the Damastown parochial house. All through the night, the frightened, frothing, sweating animal had to be continually cleaned and rubbed down. This incident had been revealed to my grandmother by the priest's man several years afterwards. The old people used to recall that the parish priest had announced from the altar at the time of the tragedy that he prayed that the murderer would not die like the dog. The gossips like to add that a man who had hurriedly left the area after the murders died in America, having, just before he died, snarled and barked three times like a dog. The old folk of centuries past had, apparently, strong imaginations.

These sordid murders could not be allowed to pass into history without attracting the antics of the local "boys" who had a crudely-printed nine verse ballad of the incident distributed at fairs and in pubs, retailing at one penny a sheet. This ballad was rendered with the gusto of a modern pop singer, regardless of the feelings and sensitivities of the victims' relatives. The ballad was headed with a crude drawing of a coffin-lid over the words "A Sorrowful Lamentation . . . ".

A SORROWFUL LAMENTATION ON
THE HOLLYWOOD TRAGEDY
WHERE TWO SISTERS HAVE BEEN
BRUTALLY MURDERED

All you who have kind feelings here with me now sympathise
It's when you hear this tale of blood it will you much surprise
Two holy sisters they were murdered all by some villain's
    hand
Such a horrid deed was never known in this our fatherland.

One Richard Murphy held a farm in Hollywood we hear
Which was held by his father William for many a long year
And to his one son Richard he willed the house and
    ground,
To his two daughters Ellen and Anne were portioned £30.

It was on a Monday evening Richard Murphy did come home
When he beheld a dreadful sight—caus'd him to sigh and
      moan.
His sister Ellen near the door lay bleeding in her gore,
Two awful wounds in her fair neck her skull was batter'd sore.

When the other sister did arrive and found them all around
It was in a field rere to the house was Anne's cold body found,
A lifeless corpse covered with blood most dismal to be seen,
It would freeze the hardest heart to see a-milking she had
      been.

Their brother was arrested and sent to Kilmainham Jail,
Compelled to stand his trial for him they'd take no bail.
On circumstances he was tried so all may plainly see,
Why the learned Judge and Jury too have set the brother
      free.

It was no stranger done this deed well every one may know,
But some bloodthirsty villain to prove their overthrow.
The money he would also take if he had only time
But Providence who rules above will yet reveal this crime.

This trial lasted seven days in Green St Court we hear
His Parish Priest and others for him they did appear.
Sidney and Curran his Counsellors, the law did expound
The Judge and Jury did agree, Not Guilty he was found.

Alas, no bloodyer deed was done in the most cruel times,
Two fine young women murdered for neither stain or crimes.
We hope all friends and neighbours will devoutly for them
      pray,
Vengeance is mine said the Lord upon the judgement day.

God help their dear relations, they now are pained in grief
By this most cruel murder; for them there's no relief,
As those two sisters were beloved by all the neighbours round,
We hope to hear before it's long of the murderer been found.

P. Brereton. Printer, 1 Lr. Exchange St., Dublin.

The widow Murphy died in 1935. With dread, I had passed her dimly-lit cottage on dark nights en route from the Five Roads to my mother's Damastown home, further terrified as her growling, snarling dog leaped forth from behind the fragile wooden gate—a vivid reminder of its predecessor of a century ago. Nothing now remains of that tragic scene—cottage and surrounds are all demolished. Forgotten now and almost unknown, under the lone yew tree in the graveyard, facing the disused lime kiln, is the trampled grave of those two sisters. Even on its crowded close October patron day, no one comes to this shaded spot to stand and breathe a silent prayer.

Our last place of interest is Saint Canice's Well, which is situated in Hollywood Great, in a field close to the Nag's Head cross-road leading to Naul village. My grandmother could recall seeing devout pilgrims crossing the fields to fetch its pure water for the curing of headaches and diseased throats. Now, it is but a dribbling, muddy, weed-choked pool, reluctantly used by thirsty, wandering cattle. It is part, however, of the ancient history of Hollywood and should not be allowed to be plodded out of existence. The story of Saint Canice is one of greatness and his scholarly writings are linked with those of the great Saint Columcille. Regrettably, he is but a vague memory to the Irish in their devout haste to honour the saints of other lands.

For many years, ancient Hollywood has lain in peaceful obscurity. Now that area may become one of the most popular in Co. Dublin, as it is expected soon that 150 acres of its fertile land will be transformed into an 18-hole golf course, which will overlook the little ruined church of Saint Canice surrounded by the graves of peaceful slumbers.